A THI[RD?] FORGIVENESS
Towards a Paradigm of Racial Justice

Ivan A. Beals

A THEOLOGY OF FORGIVENESS
Towards a Paradigm of Racial Justice

Ivan A. Beals

Christian Universities Press
San Francisco - London - Bethesda
1998

Library of Congress Cataloging-in-Publication Data

Beals, Ivan A.
   A theology of forgiveness : towards a paradigm of racial justice / Ivan A. Beals.
     p. cm.
   Includes bibliographical references and index.
   ISBN 1-57309-227-4 (hardcover : alk. paper). -- ISBN 1-57309-226-6 (pbk. : alk. paper)
   1. Forgiveness of sin. 2. Forgiveness--Religious aspects--Christianity. 3. Christianity and justice. 4. Race relations--Religious aspects--Christianity. I. Title.
BT795.B294 1998
234'.5--dc21
                                                                         98-3064
                                                                             CIP

Copyright 1998 by Ivan A. Beals

All rights reserved. Printed in the United States of America. No part of this book may be used or reproduced in any manner whatsoever without written permission except in the case of brief quotations embodied in critical articles and reviews.

Editorial Inquiries:
International Scholars Publications
7831 Woodmont Avenue, #345
Bethesda, MD 20814

To order: (800) 55-PUBLISH

Dedication

Dedicated to the Glory of God.

Acknowledgements

Dr. Jorge M.S. Barros, my brother in Christ, who helped guide this manuscript to publication.

Dr. W.E. McCumber, who has been my friend and mentor.

Jennifer Shepardson, for typing.

Isaac Abundis, for formatting the final manuscript.

Earnest Garrett, for proofreading the final manuscript.

My Daughter, Verna Jeanne, for assisting with details of publication during my illness.

Thanks to my wife, Evelyn,
and my daughters,
Verna Jeanne Heavner and Evangeline Gardner,
for living with me in a forgiving relationship.

About the Author

Dr. Ivan A. Beals was the author of nine previous books on theology, eschatology and social issues. He also edited religious journals such as "Herald of Holiness" and the "Intercultural English Projects", for Publications International.

Dr. Beals served as a pastor for the Church of the Nazarene in various locations for over a quarter of a century. A popular lecturer and preacher throughout the world, the author was also much concerned with social issues. In 1997, he published <u>Our Racist Legacy: Will The Church Resolve The Conflict?</u> He served as a member of the Mayor's Task Force on Race Relations, Justice Committee, in Kansas City, Missouri. He was also honored by an official Resolution from the Missouri House of Representatives as an "outstanding Missourian" for his efforts in addressing the problems of racism within the Church.

"Whereas, Ivan Beals suggests that individuals need to become aware of their own racist ideas and seek to deal with them in Christian love while the church needs to reevaluate its status quo position to promote understanding and reconciliation among all people."

(From the Missouri House of Representatives Resolution)

Contents

	Page
Foreword	9
Author's Preface	11
I. Mankind's Plight	13
II. Why Sin Prevails	29
III. God's Word Indicts Sin	43
IV. Redeemed from Sin unto Righteousness	59
V. Christ's Holy Atonement	75
VI. The Meaning of Jesus' Blood	91
VII. The Holy Virtue of Forgiveness	105
VIII. Forgiveness, Consecration, and Cleansing	121
IX. Our Ministry of Reconciliation	137
X. Forgiveness Heals the Hopeless	149
Bibliography	165

Foreword

The ultimate consequence of divine forgiveness is heaven. God took Ivan home to heaven before his manuscript could become a book. During my last visit with him we discussed the manuscript and its publication. Just before he died he told his daughter, Verna J. Heavner, that he wanted me to write a foreword. I am honored to comply with his wish, for we are close friends.

The church of Jesus Christ is a community of forgiven sinners. The Church is also a community of forgiving saints. Human forgiveness is necessitated by divine forgiveness. Because God has forgiven us, we must forgive others. Because God has forgiven us we *can* forgive others. His loving actions provide both the model and the power for ours.

God doesn't forgive because sin doesn't matter. He forgives because Christ has made atonement for sins--for all sins and for all time and for all persons. We forgive others, not because their sins are small or because their merits are large; we forgive for the same reason God forgives, because Christ atoned for sin. We are most Godlike when we forgive those who sin against us. The full and free forgiveness that Christ provided in His atoning death creates hope for every sinner. At the same time it forbids any of us to condemn others.

For thirteen years Ivan and I worked closely together. We also worshipped as members of the same church. I knew him to be a forgiven and forgiving man. If his book is used by the Lord to bring anyone to the liberating experiences of being forgiven and offering forgiveness, he will rejoice as one who has been handsomely paid for his labors. He wrote, not to get something off his chest, but to share something from his heart. He was subject, not object, of his writing; he wrote to help others.

—W. E. McCumber
Gainesville, Georgia
August 25, 1997

Author's Preface

"Please forgive me" becomes a reluctant person's phrase to meet the recurring need for forgiveness throughout life. The initial pardon that confessing sinners find at the cross of Jesus becomes incomplete. The full realm of forgiveness extends far beyond that. The Lord forgives us so we can be forgiving; God calls us unto a holy, forgiving fellowship.

Human sin and depravity presents a paradox—God's holy creation gone awry. The universal flaw, involving you and me, cannot be cured by any self-help efforts or innate moral virtues. Rather, God meets our plight with His forgiving grace, redemption through Jesus Christ.

I remain amazed at the price paid for forgiveness—the shed blood and death of the Lamb of God, Jesus. Our atonement with God requires the blameless sacrifice of His only begotten Son for our sins. This loving act depicts God's kiss of forgiveness upon all who believe on the Savior. We become justified before God and restored to new life in His family by His amazing grace.

Living faith in the Lord Jesus demands a sense of pardon for all past, and freedom from all present sins. Such faith gives Christ's Spirit dominion over our sins and brings peace to our hearts. The Holy Spirit's continued cleansing assures us of present pardon and power to live in obedience to Him.

This Spirit of truth ever reminds me that God's call to holy living remains a call to be forgiving—like Christ. Personal pardon and justification before God prompts us to walk in obedience to His will. Divine grace draws us to full consecration and cleansing—to be filled with the Spirit in sanctifying power made holy. He enables us to do the seeming impossible—be forgiving! Through Jesus' precious blood,

—Ivan A. Beals

CHAPTER I

Mankind's Plight

It dawned on me that something was wrong—even at the age of four. A dark, scary gap yawned between the way things were and the way I was told they ought to be. It was not easy to do as I was told. I felt pulled to disobey, though I knew I should not. One night, in a dream, I saw the devil chasing me, about to catch me. I woke up crying.

I wondered who could save me and take away the guilt I felt. God seemed to know all about me, and I hoped He would understand my needs. From my early Christian training I knew Jesus would help me—if I asked Him. That morning, Mother led me to ask God for forgiveness of my rebel will, for Jesus' sake. My child-faith reached out, and I sensed relief from the threat of the evil one. It became as though my mother had kissed away the hurt of an awful bruise.

We sometimes hear: "To err is human, to forgive divine." These words of Alexander Pope imply a human racial lack. What a person should be by God's set standards—he refuses to be. He violates the life and moral principles that are the base for human civilization. Wise people of every age have pondered this defect in mankind's nature.

The human state in terms of sin and depravity is a paradox. Few will deny the wicked conduct of mankind in the world. Why should we sin unless demons or a neurosis prompts us? Why can't we locate any fully human and humane society that is moral, just, and peaceable? Why does "man's inhumanity to man" rage unabated? Albert Outler declares, "Something has gone fearfully awry in the human enterprise."[1]

John Chrysostom, one of early Christianity's eloquent preachers, often said, "There is only one calamity—sin!"

St. Paul exclaimed, "When I want to do good, evil is right there with me. For in my inner being I see another law at work in the members of my body, waging war against the law of my mind and making me a prisoner of the law of sin at work within my members" (Rom. 7:21-23, NIV).*

Something in every man, woman, and child hates to admit any need of divine revelation. We like to feel that we are in control of our own lives, what we think and what we do. We take special pride in trying to solve the unknown that confronts and frightens us. But we reject what God has revealed as suspect and worthless because it didn't come through our ingenuity.

Frederick the Great, 18th century king of Prussia, once heard a preacher extolling the natural goodness of mankind. After a bit, King Frederick growled out, "He doesn't know this perishing human race!"

Various thinkers have explained humanity's evil ways by blaming a common cause for sin's origin. Some simply and blindly ignore the fact. Many people deny any connection with or accountability to the Almighty God, Creator. Others reject any concept of original sin and the fall of mankind from the created state of sinless innocence.

But John Fletcher, noted vicar of Madeley, declared:

> Take away the doctrine of the fall, and the tower of evangelical truth built by Jesus Christ is no more founded on a rock, but upon the sand; . . . Shall we charge the Son of God in Whom are hid all the treasures of Divine wisdom with the unparalleled folly of coming from heaven to atone for innocent creatures, . . . to deliver from the curse a people not accursed, to hang by exquisitely dolorous wounds made by His sacred hands and feet on a tree more ignominious than the gallows, for honest men, . . . and to expire under the sense of the wrath of heaven that He might save from hell people in no danger of going thither.[2]

The late Rev. Seth Joshua once told how he met a man who said he couldn't swallow what the preachers called "original sin." "My good fellow," said Rev. Joshua, "there's no occasion for you to swallow it—it's inside you already."

Cynics deny the truth of that retort. Many use mental gymnastics to avoid the reality of evil, or to reject personal blame. Moral concepts are not received as divine absolutes, but as only derived from diverse human circumstances.

Generally, non-biblical theories account for racial evil from a rationalistic viewpoint. The biblical explanation is dismissed as mythology or allegory. We should note how humanistic thought views moral evil in mankind:[3]

1. Sin becomes labeled the result of an eternal principle of evil. Both the tenets of good and evil are said to have existed eternally in endless conflict. The evil principle appears in the created material universe, to corrupt its very substance.

2. Sin becomes tagged as the limitation of mankind's finiteness. Such limits also indicate the negation or restraint of being. Since all people are finite, sin is the inevitable result.

3. Sin appears to be a necessary antagonism, assuming all life as action and reaction. There can be no good without evil. sin occurs as an impersonal law of being, which excludes personal responsibility.

4. Some people locate sin in the sensuous nature of mankind. They account for it by splitting the human person into body and soul. Because humans seek pleasure in material objects rather than in the benefits of spiritual things, this sensuous nature becomes named the source of sin.

5. Scholars from Greek philosopher Socrates to John Dewey and scholars of today have ascribed the origin of sin to ignorance. This assumes that when a person learns the truth his moral character will change. The process may be endless.

6. Sin becomes also viewed as an evolutionary lag. It remains as a bestial remnant from lower stages of existence. Sin is no more or less than the brute heritage which every person has.

7. Others regard sin as strictly social evil. Jean-Jacques Rousseau, 18th century thinker, said God made all things good, but humanity's so-called progress spoiled their morality. Socialist Karl Marx declared sin stood as unjust social inequality. One's sin rebelled against the state.

Some who admit the biblical doctrine of original sin say a person's wrongdoing follows circumstances that mold human behavior. Sin supposedly springs from other marked causes, rather than from perverted planning on mankind's part. Inexperience, ignorance, lack of self-control, and physical and social conditions become viewed as sources of human failure.

Secular humanists broadly label mankind's defiance of God as the faulty action of one who stands basically good. Our lawless bias appears as a flaw in divine creation, or as an unfortunate mishap in evolutionary growth. Some people claim sin occurs because of a lack of knowledge, or as an accidental abuse of freedom.

A terse couplet in the *New England Primer* declares:

> In Adam's fall—
> We sinned all.

Such sin twists human personality out of its divine design to live in joy and beauty forever. The world is evil, not because of the gross wickedness of a few bad people, but because of the common selfishness, prejudice, and rebellion in each of us.

A Radical Wrongness

William Allingham wrote a piercing rhyme:

> Sin, we have explained away;
> Unluckily, the sinners stay.

A universal human flaw lurks that cannot be overcome or cured by any of our self-help efforts or supposed moral virtues. Sin manifests itself in the abuse of human appetites, passions, and faculties which in themselves stand innocent. The sinful nature reigns in a person's heart until divine grace dethrones it. But this selfish, rebellious mind resists any total submission to the will of God.

Throughout time, mankind persists in all manner of selfish and violent traits. Psychologists have been forced to survey more closely the flooding stream of people's disruptive acts. This woeful display of wrongness in human behavior needs to be altered. As one has said, "We the people are the ecological problem."

Sigmund Freud, noted psychoanalyst, tried to pinpoint the human predicament. He set forth the Id, a subconscious source of a person's organic energy, from which self-centeredness and basic desires spring. Mankind's lawlessness became blamed on his Id. This raises questions about the extent a person really stands accountable for his own deeds.

For some years people shunned the topic of "personal sin." In the 1950s, when I began pastoring, such sermon subjects became banned in many church circles. Though most religious leaders confessed our world's turmoil, our failures became described as the birth pangs of a growing civilization. Life's evils would vanish as financiers solved our economic ills, with better education, higher wages, and decent housing. Such strides would surely lessen crime and violence.

Yet there exists no quick-fix kit to correct the sin problem. Many preachers have bypassed the direct reproof of the prophet—"The heart is deceitful above all things, and desperately wicked: . . . " (Jer. 17:9, KJV). Many people choose the more pleasant ground of discussing Freud's ideas about a person's "inferiority complex."

We face the temptation to rationalize in our headstrong world. But secular humanistic thought becomes muddled when mankind's revolt proves to be wrong. Consider the years of permissive attitudes and actions that began to hold sway in the 1960s. How does one explain the surging drug craze, from alcohol to marijuana, to cocaine and other mind-bending addictions? How does one explain the tragic waste of bodies on sexual perversions? How does one explain the murderous killing of fetuses in willful abortions? This broad, crowded way remains filled with suffering and dying humanity.

Such willful splurges, going against life, deny that mankind has a neutral nature or any inherent goodness. As Roger Hazelton observes, "A great and awful perversion has occurred."[4] Adam, the representative man, and all mankind, have sold his divinely created purpose to glorify the loving Creator cheap—for the plenteous stew of a power-centered and obsessed culture.

Before mankind fell, the authority behind human will was God's love, which gave a complete knowledge of the Lord God Almighty. Sovereign God created mankind with a capacity to know Him, fully aware of His love. But in a wild attempt to grab more knowledge, mankind withdrew from the light of fellowship with the Lord God. Humanity's intellect became darkened and dwarfed rather than enlightened and enlarged.

When mankind listened to the tempter's lure to evil, to assert their own will, they doubted divine love. By self parting from God, humanity lost knowledge of the Divine and squelched love for the Lord God. Selfishness became the ruling precept behind people's actions. That precept clouded their minds, debased their emotions, and degraded their wills.

G. Campbell Morgan, a biblical scholar, once declared, "Man is a ruined instrument." Yet humanity retains, in impaired form, the natural elements that comprise the Divine image. Human intellect still demands the light of knowledge. Human emotion ever seeks objects upon which to fasten, and human will requires a ruling principle. In brief, humanity demands God—without really knowing it.[5]

Having lost their knowledge of Almighty God, mankind supplants the dethroned One with other gods. The most blatant infidel, who denies a Supreme Being exists, still worships. Where there is no other object, a person enshrines himself, and bows down, vowing to create things he can comprehend. He thereby makes his own understanding the very deity that receives worship.

A person's concept of Almighty God becomes formed as one gathers from knowledge of his own personality. One can hardly think of God except by projecting the traits of human personality into infinitude. The fact the Lord God created mankind is the spiritual in a person, and confirms he is in the image of God.

On the other hand, a person creates a god on the basis of his knowledge of himself. This provides the background for the entire epic of idolatry. All false gods are distortions of the one true God, and twisted ideas are the result of the ruined image of the Lord God in mankind.

The Old Testament reveals three popular concepts of the Lord God expressed in false systems of religion—each mingled with truth. But their garbled truth works disaster. The three ideas became mounted by three words: Baal, Moloch, and Mammon. All false thinking about the Lord God Almighty clusters around those terms. Though other gods became named, they are all offspring of some aspect or attitude of those essential misconceptions.[6]

The worship of Baal deified nature. Its ritual observed the central and most marvelous fact in nature—the faculty of reproduction. All nature worship, rising from the seeming harmless adoration of the beauty and order of nature, becomes embraced by lustful sexual vice. Though Baal worship gropes for knowledge of God in nature, its search remains futile. Humanity's darkened understanding only touches the mystery of life through the power of reproduction. This misses the Divine truth of life. Without that vital contact with God's truth, one's whole being becomes degraded.

Cruel acts expressed the worship of Moloch. Its chief rite required the sacrifice of children. This debased humanity's emotional nature. When mankind magnifies their own sensations they find a god who seems to be appeased by brutal ritual. Hate thus lives next door to love. As in the worship of nature, gross conduct thrives through one's corrupt mind. The deprived and depraved affectional nature will harshly express itself, without love, in savage forms toward humanity's offspring.

Mankind still worships Moloch. Modern people has deified and bows in fearful service at the shrine of life. Its mystery involves their very offspring. But they worship with calloused heart and total indifference to the ruin wrought. Child abuse has taken on epidemic proportions in America. Hundreds of millions of socialists crowd around the shrines of bloody bodies scattered around the globe. People's lust for power spurs their worship.

Some say Mammon was the name of a Syrian god. It stood for wealth, and the power of wealth. Jesus, in the Sermon on the Mount, declared,

"You cannot serve God and Mammon [lit. Aramaic, 'riches']" (Matt. 6:24 NKJV). His words show a complete understanding of human nature and a far-sighted knowledge of the results of sin.

In all the idolatries of mankind, even civilized people, false worship issues because the race ignored God through sin. Mammon calls for the deification of human will. When one projects himself into immensity, he magnifies a will that insists on others being servile. A deity becomes worshiped whose godhead expounds mastery, and whose scepter of power holds any wealth.

The evil one often hides behind some other object of worship. Satan ever lures people to submit to his sway by dangling before them the charms of wealth and the power that it commands. Worship of riches submits to wealth, for the sake of its power, all that a person should give to God. With God's dethronement, one installs selfish desire as the ruler of his will. He thereby measures greatness as being able to master other people.

Benjamin Franklin measured human sickness when he said, "So convenient a thing it is to be a reasonable creature, since it enables one to make or find a reason for everything one has a mind to do."[7]

Rather than accept God-given responsibility, we try to manipulate reason for selfish ends. We blind ourselves when we make our rationalizations reasonable, losing sight of where we stand before the Creator. Though psychologists may term the manipulation of reason "rationalization," the Bible calls it sin. Such acts spring from the influx of evil ideas. They squelch the righteous impact of diving love and confuse what we choose to love and to hate.

Scripture defines rationalization with the term "idolatry." Alfred North Whitehead wrote, "The keynote of idolatry is contentment with the prevalent gods."[8] This remains a serious matter to us. It far exceeds the primitive habit of offering sacrifice and bowing down to idols of wood and stone. Today, idolatry assumes more subtle forms. But it has always meant putting something less than God in the place of worship belonging to Him. It causes the willful, suspicious self to turn from knowing God's will. Idolatry obliterates true love and then abuses other people.

The "Eden Catastrophe," recorded in Genesis 3, transcends human reason and experience. Scripture deals in detail with the fact of humanity's sin—its origin, curse, and penalty. A seemingly small disobedience to God by the first pair wrecked the world. All creation became caught in a treadmill of endless regression. That fateful choice threw all life—vegetable, animal, and human—out of its divine orbit. All inheritors throughout the ages have been swamped by a universe of misery. Subsequent generations have inevitably become enmeshed in the sin and fall of Adam and Eve.

Our birth into a sin-ruined world warps and twists our judgment of its serious nature. We have lost any sense of its awful sentence, the guilt of remorse and the warning of God. He withholds His final judgment, but humanity's bent to rebel follows the selfish pattern set. We ignore God's love and forgiveness, and refuse to love and forgive those who have wronged us.

Mankind's wayward mind follows the path of hatred that leads to death. Confused, wasted lives become strewn with the rubble of many idols. The human race has been blasted by the heat of bloody strife, following illusions that only lead to damnation. Our rebellious dreamland wanderings end up in the wilderness of destruction.

Yet we cannot lay the total blame of our plight on the tragic disobedience of our first parents. Though the woeful results still afflict us, and we enter this world with a bias toward evil, we retain freedom of choice God gave mankind. The same calamity that marred the Garden of Eden occurs in the life of every human being when he reaches the age of accountability. Each of us becomes morally responsible for the sinful choices we make, knowing the difference between right and wrong. We follow the same fatal course of Adam and Eve against God, and we become condemned with personal guilt. Evil thoughts and deeds distort our lives.

I once heard E. Stanley Jones clearly define evil. He said "e-v-i-l" is "l-i-v-e" spelled backwards. It is a person living his life the exact opposite of what God, the Creator, intended. Mankind thus follows the rule of evil even unto death, going against God's decrees of life and the order of nature. One's willful self-assertion to do evil counters God's loving purpose for the human race, everlasting life.

Our society's moral trouble is not because we became strayed children, as babes lost in the woods. Rather, we remain knowing sinners, a mutinous human race. Our situation stands both pathetic and tragic. This wicked world contorts our imagination to accept any human practice as normal, even though such ideas move against the order of nature. But neither denying God's truth nor whitewash can cover our great life-need, to live obedient to God.

Some psychologists admit mankind stands basically perverse. Careful analysis shows there exists no correlation between the knowledge of right and wrong and moral behavior. A study of children found that although knowledge of right and wrong increased as they became older, so did deceitfulness. This discounts the notion that lack of knowledge is the underlying problem of a human person.

Mankind's magnified self-esteem and ruinous outbreaks attest a radically sick nature. Since evil became inborn and universal, mankind stands naturally evil. Humanity needs continuous education and restraints to keep life within civil bounds. Yet, the human race hovers near the brink of self-destruction.

John Bunyan, in his *A Book for Boys and Girls*, describes the human plight in rhyme:

> From God he's a backslider;
> Of ways, he loves the wider;
> With wickedness, a sider;
> More venom than a spider;
> In sin he's a confider;
> A make-bait and divider;
> Blind reason is his guider;
> The devil is his rider.

Bunyan was right. Mankind became treacherous. One may not only ask: "Why do people go wrong?" but "How did mankind get this way?" How is a person's inbeing sin to be corrected or removed? Did God create a faulty being? If not, who or what is responsible? How is one to be restored into divine fellowship?

Scripture says the Lord God created mankind holy—in His image. But, turning from their Maker, evil people prefer almost anything over God. They indulge some aspect of life, bringing deadly harm to both physical and spiritual health. They waste their time and substance in wicked ways—seduced by selfish whims rather than seeking the righteousness of a sovereign God.

Jonathan Edwards, a fiery preacher of the 18th century, declared humanity's plight in "The Justice of God in the Damnation of Sinners." He assessed the human being as: "A little, wretched, despicable creature; a worm, a mere nothing, and less than nothing; a vile insect that has risen up in contempt against the majesty of Heaven and earth."

Our concern about a proper self-esteem shudders at such a low concept of personal mankind. Yet a vital lesson surfaces here. No person should think more highly of himself than he ought. No one stands worthy of God's favor, but His grace and pardon remain available to all. True self-esteem occurs only as we accept God's saving plan for our lives.

It seems impossible that the human soul, marred and dwarfed by sin, could ever regain God's loving purpose. Since God repeatedly commands His people to be righteous and holy, one wonders to what extent a person can be restored to do right in this perverse world. Little hope is considered because of the obvious lack of innate human goodness.

Wolfhart Pannenberg asserts that mankind lacks a direct relation to the infinite, which would enable humanity to control God. Yet they pervert their relation to God through the worship of images of finite creatures. This throws the human ego back upon itself. Unable to live in openness to God's truth, people trap themselves in the conflict between openness to God and selfhood.

Pannenberg thus says:

> Man remains imprisoned in his selfhood. He secures himself through what has been attained, or he insists on his plans. In any case, to the extent that he is able, he fits what is new into what was already in his mind. In this way not only does he readily damage his destiny to be open to the world; he also closes himself off from

the God who summons him to his destiny. The selfhood that is closed up within itself is sin.

Like Augustine, Pannenberg identifies the core of sinful self-centeredness as self-love, elevating the human ego as the final purpose toward which everything else is related. This tends to define sin more as a human structural phenomenon rather than a moral one. Since a person's selfhood becomes extensively related to his organic structure, it remains difficult to understand the manner in which one's ego is identified with sin. Pannenberg and other theologians insist: "In and of itself, selfhood is not sin, any more than control over the world—with which the ego asserts itself and prevails—is sin; . . . however, it is sin insofar as it falls into conflict with man's infinite destiny."

Yet sin became more than a structural phenomenon; it remains a basic dissolution of the divine-human relationship.

Most people sense that some deadly poison assails human life from within. It confounds all who deal with such issues from a mortal viewpoint. There are two axioms by which all theories on the origin of sin must be tested—God's pure holiness and mankind's freedom to choose. All non-biblical views fail completely in this context. The Bible reveals the only true solution to moral evil, giving the Divine remedy.

God's Reply to the Sin Question

God's Word answers the life and death issues about the origin of sin through mankind's revolt. The inspired record sets forth the disease and cure. Scripture relates mankind's moral wreck and presents the problem as restoring a person's righteousness. One must admit his moral and spiritual sickness to properly grasp God's just and ample cure.

Actually, the Old Testament does not formally define sin. Yet the scriptural evidence strongly focuses on the concept that sin is "anything contrary to the known will of God." Mankind's sinful fall, as told in Genesis 3, indicates that the human pair knew the Lord God's decree, and they were free to choose to resist or yield to temptation. Time after time human sin appears as a person refusing to worship God

Mankind's Plight

as God. Sinful people ever try to take God's place in the world, by worshiping the creature instead of the Creator, refusing to believe God.

The Bible simply says that sin entered the human race through sinful thoughts and acts of Adam and Eve. Thus sin refers to the nature of the sinner and to the sinful acts he does in opposing the will and rule of God. This destroys the fellowship of mankind with God, and brings physical and spiritual death upon the human race (cf. Rom. 6:23). Sin in its broadest sense means any transgression against the law of God. In a more specific sense, sin is choosing to disobey what one knows to be the will of God (cf. Psalm 51; Rom. 6:12-14).

Scripture refers to sin in two general respects. Sin is a matter of a person's condition, his moral state. It is also a matter of his action, what he does. Human sinfulness includes both the state of sin and the acts that stem from that sinful nature. The very traits of sin so deprave mankind that no one can restore himself to righteousness.

Despite the vile extent to which all mankind has erred, God, in mercy, loves to forgive. Though the human race became totally depraved, He can redeem. Our disobedience did not surprise the Almighty so He had no resource for a remedy. From the foundation of the world, the Savior's redeeming blood met the chance of our sin (cf. Rev. 1:5; 13:8). In the fullness of time, Christ was sent as a man among humanity, showing them God's holy way.

The gospel of God declares His matchless grace copes with mankind's sinful worst. But no saving "Rock of Ages" stands for us except we as sinners find divine forgiveness at the Savior's cross. His sacrificial act at Calvary offers both new light and new life to our blighted beings.

Mankind lost their created holy estate by making selfish choices. The human race plunged headlong into the darkness and bondage of sin. The fall did not occur because God failed to reveal himself and His will. God's revelation does not merely remain in decrees, but in the person of His Son. Jesus Christ's coming offers redemption, that transforms the heart, soul, will, and mind—the total person. Our evil ways become changed by our faith in Christ's perfect sacrifice, and we receive divine forgiveness and cleansing.

Though we do not merit God's love—He extends it. He offers us salvation because we can't help ourselves. We cannot be restored to Him by simply doing specified works. The Apostle declares, "For it is by grace you have been saved, through faith—and this not from yourselves, it is the gift of God—not by works, so that no one can boast" (Eph. 2:8-9).

No person can atone for himself. We may feel sorry for our sins and try to make amends for them, but nothing we can do will reconcile us to God. The Lord alone has the purity and power to atone and offer forgiveness. He revealed His truth and the Word became made flesh, calling us to obey His holy will.

God's inspired Word to mankind became written by people who received the inspiration of the Spirit. Through that divine gospel, our selfish hearts and arrogant minds become illumined with truth. Yet God's message does not remain beyond dispute. He did not act to redeem our world by supernatural authorship, without possible reproach. Rather, through His sacred book, applied by the Spirit, believers see God's grace revealed in His Son, Jesus. He gave himself that we might freely receive everlasting life.

Mankind and their world remain hopeless without a Redeemer. All creation depends on Him. The created magnetic poles of earth have held it in orbit around the sun and around the polar star of our universe. Yet, both physically and spiritually, the cross of Christ has kept humanity and their world from total ruin. Their salvage requires a personal choice to turn from selfishness and to trust the Divine Savior.

Within the created order God allowed freedom. How costly is that freedom! Without Jesus' shed blood, without that price paid, there is no remission, no release from our sin. Neither can a person truly find himself, or the gift of divine grace. Without the Cross there is no crown, no righteous reward, and there can be no life of victory over sin, the flesh, the devil, or death.

More than wise words became needed from God to redeem mankind from ruin. Our plight demands both divine light and redemption. God so loved that He moved throughout history to bring us salvation. In sending His Son, Jesus, the Lord God not only gave us His portrait, but His very presence.

God reconciled the world to himself, joining our plight. He came in Christ to rescue us from the bondage of sin, giving a perfect offering on the Cross.

Our sin that pierces God—that broke His heart on Calvary—is not what shocks us. We seem most repulsed by social sins that hinder the growth of human ties. Yet the evil display that wounds Almighty God is the thing we highly esteem. From the beginning we humans have preferred self-pride, one's right to himself, over obedience to the sovereign God.

Our sinful state requires the awesome power of God's holy kiss of forgiveness. Despite our pretense, we are not sages, but sinners. Though the first human pair stood created holy, rightly related to God, we face why the race rebels against God. How and why did sin flourish in mankind? The source of evil and its infection becomes traced and known to discern the necessity of God's redeeming grace.

God took the initiative, moving to provide mankind with full salvation. He didn't shrug His shoulders at sin, with a "so what" attitude. He indicts evil and its sinful results for what it is—open revolt against Him. The ensuing chapters will focus on mankind's fall into sin, and unfold the Divine plan of forgiveness and cleansing. All of Adam's race became sinners from birth—in need of a Savior.

Charles Wesley portrays the case of humanity's sin through the words of his hymn:

> Sinners turn; why will ye die?
> God, your Maker, asks you why;
> God who did your being give,
> Made you with himself to live;
> Asks the work of his own hands,
> Why, ye thankless creatures, why
> Will ye cross his love, and die?[9]

The selfish mind becomes bound to death. Its errant ways allow the ruinous blasting of confusion and the illusion of idol worship. The desolate scene of nothingness is the final fact. Without God, despair becomes both our predicament and deadly program. Our cure awaits the ending or our selfish strivings. God awaits our penitent response to His wonderful, forgiving love.

NOTES

*Unless otherwise noted, all Scripture is quoted from the New International Version of the Bible.

1. Albert C. Outler, *Theology in the Wesleyan Spirit*, (Nashville: Tidings, 1975), 29.

2. Cited by A. Paget Wilkes, *The Dynamic of Redemption*, (Kansas City: Beacon Hill Press, 1954), 25.

3. Cf. W. T. Purkiser (ed.), *Exploring Our Christian Faith*, (Kansas City: Beacon Hill Press, 1964), 224-231

4. Roger Hazelton, *Renewing the Mind*, (New York: The Macmillan Co., 1949), 7.

5. G. Campbell Morgan, *The Crises of the Christ*, (Louisville, Ky.: Pentecostal Publishing Co., 1903), 41.

6. Cf. Ibid., 43-46.

7. Cited in Hazelton, *Renewing the Mind*, 7-8.

8. Alfred North Whitehead, *Adventures of Ideas*, (New York: Macmillan Co., 1933), 12.

9. Wolfhart Pannenberg, *What Is Man? Contemporary Anthropology in Theological Perspective*, trans Duane A. Prisbe. (Philadelphis: Fortress Press, 1970), p. 13.

10. Ibid, p. 64f.

11. *Hymnal of the Methodist Episcopal Church*, (New York: Nelson & Phillips, 1878), 209-210.

CHAPTER

II

Why Sin Prevails

A little banyan seed once said to a lofty palm tree, "I am so tired of being tossed hither and thither by the wind. Let me find shelter awhile among your great leaves."

"Oh," said the palm tree, "you're welcome to light and stay as long as you wish."

So the banyan seed nestled down among the leaves of the palm tree, which soon forgot the presence of the little stranger.

The tiny seed soon sent out little roots and fibers which crept around the mighty trunk and under the bark of the palm tree. The palm tree cried out in alarm, "What is this?"

The banyan replied, "It is only the little seed you allowed to rest among your leaves."

"But now you must leave me," said the palm tree; "you are growing too large and strong to stay. You sap my strength."

"I cannot leave you now," replied the banyan, "for we have grown together. You would die if I tore myself away."

The palm tree rustled its leaves and tried to throw off the banyan, but it could not. Gradually the palm leaves withered, and the great trunk shriveled until only the banyan tree remained.

So it is with the evil root of sin within the life of a person. By one's consent, it will smother the good he might seek to do, and destroy his growth and life. Human strength and resolve alone are not able to cope with the bondage of sin, though it began as a "small matter."

The Bible says sin began as an abuse of freedom by mankind's created will. The Divine likeness created in intelligent human beings implies freedom to make moral choices, to acknowledge God's will or to disobey Him. Scripture says Adam and Eve fell when they misused that God-given freedom by willful disobedience. It marked the origin of sin.

God placed mankind on probation to receive glory by their willing service. Although God created Adam holy, he received power to choose freely between moral alternatives. Adam and Eve could choose from obedience to God's love or form willful human desires. This state granted the prospect of temptation and the possibility of sin. The choice to disobey God allowed moral pollution to enter both the personal and racial situations.

The Westminster Confession states:

> God created man male and female, with righteousness and true godliness, having the law of God written in their hearts, and power to fulfill it: and yet under a possibility of transgressing, being left to the liberty of their own will, which was subject to change.[1]

Though mankind stood created holy, certain feelings moved in every person to sin. Physical desires which, though lawful and good in themselves, could become self-directed acts of sin. Human impatience with divine providence also provoked a turning from God's will to achieve supposed good results. Sin became spawned as mankind used unjust means to gain self-righteous ends.

Genesis 3:1-4 records the historical account of mankind's probation and fall. It tells how Adam became tempted by a supernatural being, described as the serpent. This implies moral evil existed prior to its irruption in the human race. Sin became thus imported into this world from without.

The Bible infers some angels rebelled in their purely spiritual realm, and lost their first holy estate. "For if God did not spare angels when they sinned, but cast them into hell . . . " (2 Pet. 2:4, NASB; cf. Jude 6). This default in the angelic creation occurred before mankind's fall. A disrupter among the angels tempted and led them in revolt against the kingdom of God. Donald Grey Barnhouse said sin began when Satan swelled with pride and declared, "I want recognition of my worth."[2]

Scripture regards this created supernatural spirit, called Satan or the devil, as the first cause of evil. It implies he was originally good. Yet his loyalty to Almighty God became revoked as selfish thoughts of exaltation turned him against God. That mighty angel fell from his high and holy place when he became God's foe (cf. Rev. 12:7-9).

Lucifer (KJV), the "morning star" mentioned by Isaiah (14:12-15) is a name used to explain Satan's fall. Lucifer said, "I will . . . ." This is the shortest possible definition of sin in terms of its most hideous aspect. He wanted to be like God—apart from God. Lucifer began saying, "Abdicate, God—I want to sit on the throne!"

The grossness of Satan's sin appears only dimly revealed. Yet even the vague outline of his revolt unveils the summit of all sin—willful, conscious, spiritual evil. Satan was neither trapped nor deceived. He rebelled against God with clear intent and knowledge of what he began doing. He sought the power of God through pride in his own being. Of Lucifer, God said through the prophet, "Nevertheless you will be thrust down to Sheol" (Isa. 14:15, NASB).

All creation became afflicted by sin and wickedness because of the evil one's corruption.

The Steps to Shame

Thomas a Kempis once wrote: "Sin is first a simple suggestion, then a strong imagination, then delight, then assent."[3] The Bible records personal sin as much worse in its consequences than in its intentions. Sin often becomes portrayed as a deadly trap in a seemingly harmless setting.

Throughout Scripture, the Genesis account of mankind's creation and fall stands as historical truth. Other Old Testament passages plainly allude to that fall. "Have I covered my transgressions like Adam, by hiding my iniquity in my bosom . . . ?" (Job 31:33, NASB; cf. Hos. 6:7).

In the New Testament, Jesus refers to mankind's fall when He says, "Have you not read, that He who created them from the beginning made them male and female . . . ?" (Matt. 19:4-5, NASB). Christ also identifies unbelievers who do not love Him as being children of the devil (cf. John 8:44).

The apostle Paul regards mankind's fall as a real transaction, saying, "But I am afraid that just as Eve was deceived by the serpent's cunning, your minds may somehow be led astray from your sincere and pure devotion to Christ . . . . for Satan himself masquerades as an angel of light" (2 Cor. 11:3, 14; cf. 1 Tim. 2:13-15).

Scripture never hints that God is the author of evil. Indeed, God in Christ created all things (Col. 1:16). But the Lord God didn't create sin; it is not a creation. Oswald Chambers rightly defines sin as "the outcome of a relationship which God never ordained, a relationship set up between the man God created and the being God created who became the devil."[4]

Holy Writ gives two basic factors to disclose the origin of sin in the human family. First, we are told of the prior existence of evil raised in the rebel-person, Satan, who later tempted man to sin. "The great dragon was hurled down—the ancient serpent called the devil, or Satan, who leads the whole world astray" (Rev. 12:9). Second, mankind appears to have freedom of choice in the presence of moral options. A person may choose from two basic backgrounds: the love of God, or the love of self.

God created Adam innocent. God wanted him to develop as a human person through obedience. Compliance with the Divine will required the sacrifice of certain aspects of humanity's natural life to transform it into spiritual life. This would occur by a series of proper moral choices, evidently in a probationary setting. Obedience meant everlasting life. Disobedience would bring impending death.

Adam switched from God's plan of life and being. Instead of depending on God, he assumed rule over himself, and ushered sin and rebellion into our world. In this sense, "Sin is not wrong doing, it is wrong being, deliberate . . . independence of God."[5]

The Bible describes Adam's fall, showing how he, created in the moral image of God, pure and holy, disobeyed and became cursed to die. Sin thus began as a willful act against God, within the bounds of mankind's free agency. The resulting moral pollution remains both simple and complex.

As a morally responsible person, one could choose for or against God. The serpent, an incarnation of Satan, became allowed to infuse the element of temptation. However, he could only affect motives that the man and woman would at sometime feel in their probationary status. Adam fell, taking of the Divine restriction—the forbidden fruit of the tree of knowledge of good and evil.

Satan snared Adam through Eve's curiosity. The man stood as the legal racial representative. Eve's role in the fall displays three basic motives for sin: (1) physical craving, (2) intellectual desire, and (3) self-assertion. Neither Adam nor Eve cared enough about God to do His will.[6] They not only failed to acknowledge Him as their Creator, but also denied Him a true response to His love.

Scripture traces the steps to shame. The first was: "When the woman saw that the fruit of the tree was good for food and pleasing to the eye, . . . " (Gen. 3:6). The tempter used Eve's bodily senses and normal physical cravings to entice her from steadfast faith in God. This order of temptation becomes set in motion within every person's life.

The next step of intellectual desire occurs in the same verse: "and also desirable for gaining wisdom." But Eve didn't become challenged to a genuine quest for God's truth. Her impulse moved with a hasty passion to experience the fullness of life as an irresponsible and uncontrolled child. Such wisdom at first only seeks to know what is out in the world. On the one hand, eager curiosity stands essential to human development and to the progress of civilization. Yet it becomes charged with moral quality as one forsakes God to exhaust the cosmos on himself.

The third step away from God became prompted by subtle doubt of His Word, urging self-assertion. The sly serpent asked the self-seeking woman: "Did God really say, 'You must not eat from any tree in the garden'?" (v. 1).

After Eve's correct reply, the serpent tells her, "You will not surely die . . . For God knows that when you eat of it your eyes will be opened, and you will be like God, knowing good and evil" (vv. 4-5). This denial of God's rightful reign impelled them to strive for divine equality. That first human pair simply began the racial role of "playing God."

Satan's temptation also applied social pressure. Adam and Eve became a unit in the utmost sense. One cannot sin alone. Though each maintained his own free moral agency, it remains unthinkable that one should fall from God without the other. From the beginning, sin became more than a personal matter. It became also a social disease infecting the whole human race. After Eve transgressed, partaking of the forbidden fruit, "She also gave some to her husband, who was with her, and he ate it" (v. 6).

Who bears the greater blame for the fall, the man or the woman? Eve became deceived when the serpent tempted her. But Adam succumbed to disobey through his spouse's influence, knowing the bitter results. Both allowed their safeguards to temptation to be broken down. Shielding gates such as: faith, guarded by mind; love, guarded by affection; and obedience, guarded by will, became shattered.

All temptation begins in the mind. What God had said should have been received as truth by the intellects of Adam and Eve. If Eve had believed God and had affirmed her faith, she would not have yielded to temptation. But the moment doubt captured her mind, from her assent to Satan's questions, God's truth became clouded. Growing distrust subdued her faith.

When Eve saw the tree for herself, it seemed to confirm what the tempter claimed. That he disputed God's Word didn't matter. With the support of her senses and the consent of her mind, Eve both forsook faith and misplaced her love. A self-assertive search for truth became more important to her than faithful love for the Lord God.

The bulwark of love had been formed to say, "God's fellowship in the cool of the day is the sweetest and most valuable thing in my life—I will not covet more than He has given." Trust in God includes the element of love which accepts His motives as good. True love always desires to please its object, and loyal affections guard it for the Divine will and way.

But Satan said: "You will be like God." Was God depriving them of something good? Eve allowed the seed of distrust to flourish, and her love for God became deadened by suspicion and selfish ambition. Eve's love shifted from God-centeredness to self-centeredness. Her idolatrous pride rejected God's approval as the supreme value in life. The transfer of love to self meant separation from the sovereign God. Pride always wants more than the Lord God has given.

The third defense—obedience, guarded by will—also toppled. Unbelief refused God's Word as truth, and pride denied God's approval as the highest value. Will then rebelled against Divine authority and went its own way. Rather than remain obedient to the Lord God, the self-wills of Adam and Eve declared, "Even if God is right—no matter the outcome—I want my way!" Up to the point of asserting self-will, disobedience could have been shunned. Instead, Adam and Eve conceived the thought of the sinful heart—"No one can tell me how to run my life."

The Bible reveals that human nature adopts a fatal suspicion of God. It began when two primal creatures of God, the fallen angel who became the tempter, Satan, and Adam arranged a bargain that God never sanctioned. It fostered a perverse league that only God's great grace and powerful forgiveness can break.

An Ongoing Choice

Humanity's engrossment with sin becomes somewhat like this nature fable. A king went into his garden and found to his surprise wilted and dying trees, shrubs, and flowers. It was a tragic scene of spoiled beauty. Asking the oak tree the cause of its withering he learned that it started dying because it could not be tall like the pine. Turning to the pine, the king heard that it drooped because it became unable to bear grapes like the vine. And the vine said it started dying because it could not blossom like the rose.

Sin greatly infected God's earthly garden with a similar chain-like effect. Doubt, suppressing faith, tripped the first pair to fall. Self-centered affections raised human pride above God, which catered to a rebel will that chose its own way over the Divine holy purpose. That woeful reaction still continues in human lives today.

The essence of human sin does not occur as the helpless repetition of Adam's act. Neither is sin our actual misdeeds, nor even the evil drives that linger in the murky depths of the human heart. "Sin, in its essence, is human overreach—the reckless abuse of our distinctive human outreachings and upreachings—those aspirations that make us human but whose corruptions make us less than truly human."[7] In reality, "Sin is mutiny against God's rule; not vileness of conduct, but red-handed anarchy."[8]

Perhaps Adam's sin did not at first become a conscious revolt against God. Yet it soon became so and worked out that way through the human race. Rather than being the peak of all sin, Adam's sin remains at the root. Whatever sin we indulge, we become involved in the traits of the first sin. It remains as the source and the disposition of the infused suspicion: "Did God really say, . . . ?" (Gen. 3:1-5).

That first pair's fall brought immediate dire results. They parted from God only to be enslaved by evil. One "little" act broke their fellowship and shattered their peace. Yielding to Satan's temptation bound them to his revolt against God's righteous reign. Coupled with the loss of divine favor, they and their progeny became captives of physical and moral corruption. Their lives received the curse of death.

The apostle Paul uses the phrase, "a spirit of slavery" (Rom. 8:15, NASB) to define sin. The human defect and this bondage became paired metaphors for every person's abuse of his potential for creative freedom. The tragic results of such perversion rage within the fragile texture of a humane society. The ruin seems both senseless and inevitable.

No divine purpose compelled the human race to depart from what God meant us to be, to become the sinful creatures we are. No good reason can be raised to show why our "outreach" must "overreach" itself. We, as sinners, stand without excuse. Paul calls this the "mystery of lawlessness" (2 Thess. 2:7, NASB), which compares with "the mystery of godliness" (1 Tim. 3:16).

Our calamity lies in the devious welter of aspirations that corrupt each other. The modern sacrosanct Pelagian litany, "I'm O.K.—You're O.K.!" cannot silence the primal cry of sinful man, as exclaimed by the prophet, " 'Woe to me,' I cried, 'I am ruined . . . ' " (Isa. 6:5). Paul declared the example of his struggle with sin, "Wretched man that I am! Who will set me free from the body of this death?" (Rom. 7:24, NASB).

Scripture denies the Pelagian claim that our sin consists in doing as Adam did. Pelagius, early British monk and theologian, believed every person is born in the same condition as Adam, with the native capacity to sin or not to sin—as he chooses. Universal sin became explained as the effect of an unbroken chain of evil example upon the human race. Modern versions of this error have blurred a clear vision of sin.

Scripture declares the origin of sin in the human race occurred by the previous default of Satan, who tempted mankind to sin, and by personal free choice. God cannot be condemned as the Creator of evil even though He created both humans and angels with the ability to choose evil. Mankind himself became liable for the origin of sin when he chose to abuse his freedom and rebel against God.

Mankind allowed his own idol-self to usurp control of his life. Any attempt to be like God apart from God becomes sinful. Sin always exalts self in pride. Self becomes Satan's citadel in the human heart, the stronghold of the arch-enemy of the indwelling Holy Spirit. John Wesley rightly declared, "But worse than all my foes I find the enemy within."[9]

"Original sin" defines the corruption of a person's heart. It remains a universal state which defiled the entire human race as well as the individual. Though people wonder how this depravity entered the world and infected all of Adam's race, the fact remains. Wickedness lurks in the human nature as a stark reality and curse. It is like a wild monster that avoids human attempts to oust or slay that enemy.

Christian art has portrayed the spirit of evil by the figure of a basilisk. The basilisk represents a reptile which grew to a huge size, having the body of a cock, depicting sleepless vigilance. Its tail, composed of three serpents, suggested diabolical cunning. Its beak and claws of brass made it callous and cruel. The glance of the basilisk meant death. The only way to vanquish it was to hold a mirror, so that by seeing itself, the foul beast would die in horror.

Before we can loathe sin in our lives, we must see it as it exists. Rather than at once striking people dead, sin blinds its victims. When we heed God's truth our eyes become opened, we see ourselves, and receive His pardon and saving grace. Only then can sin's death-grip be broken. This issue confronts every person. The mirror of God's truth will either be the means of one's life or death.

Adam's sin did not die with him. Sin remains a corporate corruption—not a spiritual disease confined to remote victims or weak members of the human race. We all remain connected through a common life-root—like runners in a strawberry bed. Evil pollution flows through that fallen root system. We become caught up in the selfishness of society, biased against God's will for our lives.

Like the banyan seed, the sin that began as a minute sprout of doubt soon grew to a fatal tangle. Not only were Adam and Eve cast out of the holy garden "to live on their own," but their selfishness turned violent. Cain, their firstborn, killed his brother, Abel, in a jealous rage.

Adam and Eve had fully known the guilt of sin, and tried to hide from the Lord God. He killed animals to cover their nakedness, showing the plan of sin-sacrifice (Gen. 3:21). The deadly disaster of their sin became exposed, as death became the nagging curse. God only started and approved a sacrifice system that confessed the blameless character of a life-giving offering.

The Conflict of Faith and Doubt

Someone has said, "Self-preservation is the first law of nature; self-sacrifice the highest rule of grace." From the beginning, a person's dealing with Almighty God called for a life of trust in and complete obedience to Him. He does not sanction the doubt-inspired "self-saving" sacrifice, or the proud concept of "self-saving" grace.

Abel offered a sacrifice "of the firstborn of his flock," which God accepted. Cain merely offered a sacrifice comprised of the crops he had raised and gathered. That did not please God. The offering neither complied with God's sovereign will nor recognized sin as a death-dealing matter (cf. Gen. 4:2-5).

The Scripture implies Abel was both depraved and defiled by sin. Yet his faith became inspired by obedience to God's plan. Though Abel had sinned, he received salvation by divine forgiveness and grace because of his sacrifice by faith. "By faith Abel offered a better sacrifice than Cain did. By faith he was commended as a righteous man, when God spoke well of his offerings" (Heb. 11:4).

When envy stirred Cain to murder his brother, the stain of sin flowed in primal horror. A rampant tangle of evil soon covered the earth (Gen. 6:5-11). As the population increased, evil's tumult multiplied through seven generations. God saw "how great man's wickedness on the earth had become, and that every inclination of the thoughts of his heart was only evil all the time" (v. 5).

Noah, ninth from Adam, became noted as a righteous man who walked with God, "blameless among the people of his time" (v. 9). Yet this doesn't mean he had no taint of original sin. Not even the Flood could wash away the effects of the fall upon the human race. At Noah's burnt offering after the Flood, the Lord said: "Never again will I curse the ground because of man, even though every inclination of his heart is evil from childhood. And never again will I destroy all living creatures, as I have done" (Gen. 8:21).

This passage declares the total depravity of mankind in general, and that corruption appears as typical in human nature. Such an evil inclination does not merely erupt in certain periods of a person's life. It applies during one's entire history—"from childhood"—the earliest time of his accountability.[10] Neither is there any escaping the effects of evil by longevity of life.

Scripture gives no hint that depravity becomes acquired by education, a model, or otherwise. If an evil nature were not innate, it could not be traced "from childhood." Neither could such an avowal be made of mankind, or human essence. The good example and precepts of a righteous family fail to preserve their children in the faithful way or to prevent their offspring from falling into moral pollution. Even Noah, "blameless among the people of his time," set the stage for the cursing of Canaan, his grandson. Noah's drunken and naked state was an occasion of remorse for both of them (cf. Gen. 9:20-25).

God remained ever present with humanity, giving precepts and promises, warning against sin, and granting blessings from obedience. In faithful response, Job manifested forgiveness to his three accusing "comforters" by praying for them. After that, God blessed Job and gave him more than ever before his testing (cf. Job 42). But generally mankind's evil bias became stronger than moral restraints. The tide of iniquity surged beyond all barriers and re-infested the world. Divine judgment issued forth in both blessing and cursing (cf. Gen. 9:25-27).

Human history became glutted with moral and religious institutions. They developed in the calling of Abram, and the Divine law-giving through Moses. The Lord God faithfully dealt with His chosen people, the children of Abraham, Isaac, and Jacob. But the disease of sin became divulged in the rebel-nature of Israel. Their history exposes a persistent malady of the human heart. Despite the Divine promises and the wonder of prophetic fulfillment, the Israelites often strayed from the truth, pursuing their inheritance.

Even their remembrance of divine deliverance from Egyptian bondage became short-lived. At Sinai, while Moses was on the mount receiving the Ten Commandments, they fashioned and worshiped a golden calf, a god of their own design. The Lord God struck the people with a plague because of what they did (cf. Exodus 32).

Even after they became settled in the Promised Land, rather than have God rule over them, Israel wanted a human king like their pagan neighbors (1 Sam. 8:10-22). Though God's leadership always brought success, Israel resisted His sovereign authority. It stood too restrictive of their selfish interests and acts.

Only a few men stand out from the line of kings, who did God's will. Even the specially anointed reign of David became blighted. His regular lineage became eventually cut off in disgrace and captivity. Yet the Messianic hope depended on the descendants of that strain of human life.

We may rightfully observe that if mankind had a responsive moral and religious nature, there would have been fixed obedience to do God's will. No such result occurred. Despite the most powerful divine manifestations, there have been frequent revolts. Such an ongoing rebellion shows an upright nature became absent. It confirms an active evil disposition thwarting moral and religious functions.[11]

God spoke through the prophet Isaiah and said of chosen Israel: "For I knew how stubborn you were; the sinews of your neck were iron, your forehead was bronze. Therefore I told you these things long ago; . . . that you could not say, 'My idols did them; my wooden image and metal god ordained them' " (48:4-5).

God's redemptive plan for mankind became clearer with the advent of God's only Son, Jesus Christ. Jesus' life and ministry challenged mankind with a crucial life-death decision. But cruel rebuff prevailed instead of a ready response to divine truth that pointed to forgiveness and saving grace. Mankind fiercely cried for the crucifixion of the Son sent of God. His glorious revelation became labeled blasphemy.

Rebellion to the truth has raged throughout succeeding Christian centuries. When Stephen, a deacon of the Early Church, indicted the Jews for their revolt against God, they stoned him to death. In a sense, Stephen's charge became directed not only for the Jews, but for all mankind. "You stiff-necked people, with uncircumcised hearts and ears! You are just like your fathers: You always resist the Holy Spirit!" (Acts 7:41).

Mankind's endless resistance to God does not always react in furious revolt against His moral restraints. People also meet such standards as a reservation within those who may verbally accept the truth, but whose lives do not produce the fruit. Indeed, only a native aversion to a true religious life could void so many constraining forces. The guilt incurred becomes both real and damning.[12]

Lord Byron, in his Prayer of Nature, asks:

> Father of Light! Great God of Heaven!
> Hear'st thou the accents of despair?
> Can guilt like man's be e'er forgiven?
> Can vice atone for crimes by prayer?

It seems beyond our grasp to either forgive or to expect forgiveness for our sin. Simple justice demands an eye for an eye—a tooth for a tooth in any wrongdoing. Thankfully, divine judgment comes tempered with grace and mercy. Amidst God's indictment of our sin, He provides the Savior, who comes to graciously forgive and redeem us from a sinful life.

NOTES

1. Cited by H. Orton Wiley and Paul T. Culbertson, *Introduction to Christian Theology* (Kansas City: Beacon Hill Press, 1957), 162.

2. Cited by Dwight Hervey Small, *The High Cost of Holy Living* (Westwood, N.J.: Fleming H. Revell Co., 1964), 63.

3. Frank S. Mead (ed.), *The Encyclopedia of Religious Quotations* (Old Tappan, N.J.: Spire Books, 1976), 610.

4. Oswald Chambers, *The Psychology of Redemption* (London: Marshall, Morgan & Scott Ltd., 1955), 11.

5. Oswald Chambers, *Conformed to His Image* (London: Marshall, Morgan & Scott Ltd., 1955), 16.

6. Cf. Olin A. Curtis, *The Christian Faith* (Grand Rapids: Kregel Publications, 1956), 195-198.

7. Albert C. Outler, *Theology in the Wesleyan Spirit*, 40.

8. Oswald Chambers, *Conformed to His Image*, 17

9. Cited in Dwight Hervey Small, *The High Cost of Holy Living*, 64.

10. Thomas N. Ralston, *Elements of Divinity* (Nashville: Southern Methodist Publishing House, 1876), 130-131.

11. Cf. John Miley, *Systematic Theology* (New York: Hunt & Eaton, 1892) I, 460.

12. Ibid., 461.

CHAPTER III

God's Word Indicts Sin

In 1790, the crew of the "Bounty" mutinied, seized control of the vessel, and set their officers adrift. Nine of the mutineers, with 6 men and 12 women of Tahiti, landed on an uninhabited shore known as Pitcairn's Island. One of them learned how to make an alcoholic drink from roots. That remote spot, only seven miles around, became a hell from the drink. Their paradise suffered ruin from a sequence of devilish orgies and bloody massacres. By 1800, within 10 years of their landing, all the Tahitian men and all but one of the Englishmen perished.

The lone English survivor, named John Adams, had found a Bible in the wreck of the "Bounty." He read it and became struck with remorse for his crimes. He began to teach the Tahitian women and their children from it, and became the head of a patriarchal community. Though half-caste and the offspring of mutineers and murderers, the settlement became known throughout the world for its virtue. Total ruin was averted by the plain teaching of the Bible about mankind's sin.

Soren Kierkegaard reminds us, "The Bible is a book with our address on it." Both the inspired Word and the history of our human race affirm worldwide sin. The depravity of mankind stems from the fall of Adam. That native corruption, with its evil bent, becomes the only rational account of cosmic sin. Adam's sin became all mankind's sin, and the Scripture indicts it as such an ongoing source.

The Bible never glosses over or tries to explain away the evil of sin. Scripture's truthful method counters that of common writers and artists. When Alexander, the Macedonian conqueror, had his portrait drawn, he sat with his face resting on his fingers, as though in profound thought. But he posed that way to hide an ugly scar. The Bible reveals the full image of a person in severe detail—scars and all. Righteousness remains exalted and sin becomes condemned.

We may note Biblical explanations of "original sin" from two aspects: (1) the scriptural terminology of sin; and (2) specific accusations. The nature and development of sin has deeply stained humanity's personal life and marred racial history. A survey of scriptural terms reveals the wrongness of human acts and attitudes.

The Scriptural Terminology of Sin

A bad life becomes the only human objection raised against the Bible. Scripture uses plain, pointed words to describe and define sin that condemns mankind. Its word-pictures indict mankind of wrongdoing against God, others, and himself. More inwardly, God's word depicts a human bent to sin that stems from the fall.

People often ask: "In what way were all people depraved and guilty in Adam?" The Bible doesn't offer a clear-cut answer without a survey of the terms used to express the concept of sin. Old Testament terms for sin may be summarized by two lines of meaning. Some scholars say, in one instance it became failure to hit, or to conform to any objective standard. The other case relates an attitude taken by a person toward one who was his sovereign.[1]

The general Old Testament concept of sin is that of revolt, asserting self-authority. Sin stands against Almighty God the person, not simply shunning His will or breaking His law. Sin appears as the willful insolence of an individual, nation, or race against God's sovereign rule. It becomes also viewed as an evil state or condition that persists.

Aside from the New Testament terms describing our sin, many people become concerned how this affects our self-concept. Some say mankind becomes troubled enough in having proper self-esteem without adding the burden of racial guilt. Others refrain from calling misdeeds or wrongs sins.

But one's self-concept cannot be really bolstered by refusing to face sin. Sooner or later, those who ignore the reality of evil must deal with shattered illusions and destroyed lives.

The Scripture not only condemns mankind's sin, but it offers forgiveness and cleansing through divine grace though none deserves God's favor. The awful truth a person faces about his sinful self meet the holy righteous cure the Lord God provides. No one will not be pronounced guilty without the offer of redemption. To bypass the truth about God's judgment of sin becomes far more harmful and fatal to a person than naming sin for what it really is.

The Old Testament stands as a base for New Testament words used to denote sin. Several basic Greek terms depict sin as inherent depravity:[2]

1. *Hamartia* designates sin as transgression against God. It means "missing the mark," and refers to an act of personal responsibility. Sin becomes viewed as such acts when Jesus said, "Son, your sins are forgiven" (Mark 2:5b).

James writes, "But if you show favoritism, you sin (*harmartian*) and are convicted by the law as lawbreakers" (2:9). Sin also includes attitudes and inner responses.

2. The term *adikia* defines sin as unrighteousness, wickedness, or injustice. Paul says God's wrath becomes revealed against the unrighteousness (*adikian*) of people (Rom. 1:18). Among the sins listed as characteristic of the corrupt mind (vv. 19-32), unrighteousness tops the traits of mankind.

3. Sin becomes also conveyed by *anomia* as "acts or manifestations of lawlessness." It may refer to a lawless act or a lawless person, in defiance of the law and not by ignorance of it. Scripture contrasts such lawlessness with righteousness and holiness: "For just as you presented your members as slaves of uncleanness, and of lawlessness leading to more lawlessness (*anomia*), so now present your members as slaves of righteousness for holiness" (Rom. 6:19b, NKJV). Sin as lawlessness becomes a pattern of evil conduct, in endless revolt against God.

4. Sin appears as perverted desire. The term *epithumia* denotes strong desire, but its moral character becomes set by how it becomes used. James infers that desire becomes the springboard for sin: "But each one is tempted when, by his own evil desire, he is dragged away and enticed" (1:14).

Paul presents the relation of the law to wrong desire in Rom. 7:7, where the law judges dormant desire and regards it as sin. Of Paul's reference, scholars say desire should not be limited to the sensual or sexual realm. Wrong desire includes a sweeping sense of a mania for self-assertion against the claim of the sovereign God. This is the nerve of every kind of sin, from the primal flouting of God (Rom. 1:21) to sexual perversion, antisocial crimes, and all sinning met with divine punishment.[3]

5. The term *kakia* becomes used in a wholesale manner. It defines sin as wickedness as opposed to virtue, and as an evil nature. Thayer's translation gives the word two shades of meaning. First, it means malignity, malice, ill will, desire to injure (Rom. 1:29; Eph. 4:31; Col. 3:8; Titus 3:3; Jas. 1:21; 1 Pet. 2:1). Second, it means "wickedness," "depravity" (1 Cor. 5:8; 14:20; Acts 8:22). It becomes explained as wickedness that exploits freedom to break the laws (1 Pet. 2:16). Sin is a state as well as an act.[4]

6. Sin becomes a deliberate pattern of irreverence. The word *asebia* is sometimes translated "ungodliness." Paul warns: "But avoid worldly and empty chatter, for it will lead to further ungodliness" (2 Tim. 2:16, NASB). Ungodliness and unrighteousness became the two sides of sin. Irreligion parades immorality (violating the norm of right), and immorality is the token of irreligion (opposing God).[5] The Lord discerns these aspects in every sin.

7. *Parabasis* also denotes sin as a transgression. It comes from the root word *parabaino* which means to cross the line, to transgress, and to depart or desert (Acts 1:25). This usage labels sin an affront, a deliberate violation. As with Adam's sin, the term means the breach of a proclaimed, confirmed law (Rom. 5:14).

Most of us try to plead innocence rather than admit any sinful crisis. But it becomes useless to claim we remain blameless when Jesus puts His finger on our need. He says, from within a person, "out of the heart come evil thoughts, murder, adultery, sexual immorality, theft, false testimony, slander" (Matt. 15:18).

One might say, "That is nonsense—I don't have any of those things in my heart. I am innocent!" Yet sooner or later, you and I will be thrown into circumstances that will prove our claim to innocence was a figment of our imagination. Jesus told the tragic truth about the human heart.

Paul explains that the law will make mankind aware of transgression (Rom. 4:15; 5:20; Gal. 3:19). By this awareness the consciousness of sin becomes increased and the desire for redemption aroused. Viewed objectively, *parabasis* denotes sin as infringement of a known rule of life.

A study of biblical terms shows the word "sin" includes two things. First, it refers to outward acts that do not conform to divine law. Such failure displays the attitude of willful violation. Second, sin involves a subjective condition of rebellion, antagonism, corrupt desire, and willful preference of evil.

The Bible not only charges human sin as an act; it indicts sin as a state within one's personality. That corrupt plight consists of those attitudes, dispositions, and desires that lead to willful transgression. Various scriptures have been noted that trace mankind's depravity from the fall. We next turn to the concept of sin as inherited depravity.

Accused of Sin

Augustine once cried in prayer, "Oh Lord, that I might die lest I die!" We either die to self and its false claims, or we die in self before the truth that is of God. There is no neutral position for a person to hold.

God's Word asserts mankind remains born in a state of spiritual death. God gives full divine pardon unto life, forgiving the guilt and blame for which a person can not be directly responsible. But one does remain liable for the consequences of original sin; God calls each of us to yield to the cleansing of His Holy Spirit.

Perhaps the first passage that indicts mankind for having an inherited depraved nature is: "Adam . . . became the father of a son in his own likeness, according to his image" (Gen. 5:3, NASB). A contrast became drawn between the holy likeness of God and Adam's depraved image in which his son became born. In Genesis 8:21, mankind became condemned because the intent of his heart remained evil from his youth. Job then asks: "Who can bring what is pure from the impure? No one!" (14:4). This implies that every person born of the human race becomes defiled by sin.

David's prayer further pinpoints mankind's innate problem of sin. He not only seeks pardon for lying, deceit, adultery, and murder. Pleading his awful guilt, he also wants purity within. David admits: "Behold I was brought forth in iniquity, and in sin did my mother conceive me" (Psa. 51:5, NASB).

The conviction of sin increased to include more than what he had done, but what he was by nature. As David, we all become shaped in iniquity and conceived in sin. Sinful trends and passions become rooted in a racial pollution. This aspect of mankind's liability issues in one's descent from a fallen race.

Mankind's natural depraved state stands defined: "No, in your heart you devise injustice, . . . Even from birth the wicked go astray; from the womb they are wayward and speak lies" (Psa. 58:2-3). Some scholars say the words used in this passage cannot refer to actual sin. The clear meaning refers to a perverse nature from the very outset of life. It suggests a turning from God at birth.[6]

God's perfect holiness revealed to Isaiah both raised the Divine majesty and exposed the prophet's sinful nature. Isaiah confessed and cried, "Woe is me, for I am ruined! / Because I am a man of unclean lips, / And I live among a people of unclean lips, / For my eyes have seen the King, the Lord of hosts" / (6:5, NASB). The prophet beheld the greater problem—he was a corrupt man who belonged to a corrupt people and a fallen race.

The Divine Word also indicts mankind through the prophet Jeremiah. "The heart is deceitful above all things, and desperately wicked; who can know it?" (17:9, KJV). Some scholars declare that the prophet, speaking of the heart of man, points to the race in general, in its native state. Jeremiah speaks of it as totally depraved—"desperately wicked."[7]

New Testament scriptures indicting original sin are too numerous to review in their entirety. We only note some key verses. Jesus accused the morally depraved nature of mankind when He declared:

> For from within, out of men's hearts, come evil thoughts, sexual immorality, theft, murder, adultery, greed, malice, deceit, lewdness, envy, slander, arrogance and folly, All these evils come from inside and make a man unclean (Mark 7:21).

Christ asserts a new birth stands required to fit mankind for the kingdom of God. He says, " . . . unless a man is born of water and the Spirit, he cannot enter the kingdom of God. Flesh gives birth to flesh, but the Spirit gives birth to spirit" (John 3:5-6). Scholars claim the word "flesh" refers to more than one's physical being at his birth into the world. It also implies his moral condition becomes such that he needs a spiritual new birth.[8]

Paul's writings often use "flesh" to denote native corruption in mankind. One has said, "No Christian ever had a deeper sense of heart depravity or of divine deliverance from it than the apostle Paul."[9] The Apostle lists the sinful traits of mankind's debased mind, and declares sin as worldwide (Rom. 1:18-32). He asserts that people have no excuse "since what may be known about God is plain to them, because God has made it plain to them" (v. 19). Any willful rejection of the truth plants a great loathing of God within one's heart. On the other hand, when Paul tells of beating his body and making it his slave (1 Cor. 9:27), he does not allude to the flesh, the sinful mind. He refers to his innocent bodily appetites that must be controlled.

The Apostle charges that both Jews and Greeks are under sin (Rom. 3:9). "There is no one righteous, not even one" (v. 10; cf. Isa. 53:1-4; Psa. 14:1-3). "There is no difference, for all have sinned and fall short of the glory of God" (Rom. 3:23). Paul concludes sin is universal—Adam originated it, and he generated it to all humanity. The Apostle declares: "Through one man sin entered into the world, and death through sin, and thus death spread to all men, because all sinned" (Rom. 5:12, NKJV). In that chapter, he further states: "By the one man's offence death reigned through one" (5:17, NKJV). "By one man's disobedience many were made sinners" (v. 19, NKJV). "Sin reigned in death" (v. 21, NKJV).

We stand condemned in God's sight because of personal acts of sin, and through an individual link with Adam as the racial head. Paul recalled Adam's disobedience and said, "By one man sin entered into the world!" That tragedy extends from an evil nature to sinful acts. The Scripture clearly reveals something that Paul calls SIN as distinct from sins. Inborn as a principle or power, sin stands distinct from sins, the acts or fruits of sin.[10]

One may note that Paul (Rom. 5:12—8:10) uses *hamartia* for sin 40 times. The term becomes almost always used in the singular number and usually with the definite article (*he*, the). This describes sin as more than an act. It appears as an irresistible power that controls mankind, making him a helpless slave.[11]

Paul opens chapter 6 with the question: "What shall we say then? Are we to continue in sin that grace might increase?" (NASB). He obviously refers back to his statement: "but where sin increased, grace abounded all the more" (5:20, NASB). It may be pointed out that Paul does not ask, "Shall we continue to sin that grace may abound?" but, "Shall we continue in (the) sin?" It seems the question is not, shall we continue to practice sin, but shall we continue in the principle of sin?[12]

The Apostle personifies sin through a succession of Greek cases. First, it becomes the sphere and the personal object of mankind's action. It then becomes a possessing agent that seeks control. Finally, sin acts as a power that rules over mankind as his master (Rom. 6:12).

Spiritual progress begins when we realize we cannot compel the sinful self to live a Christian life. The apostle Paul declares, "For we know that our old self was crucified with him [Christ] so that the body of sin might be rendered powerless, that we should no longer be slaves to sin—because anyone who has died has been freed from sin" (Rom. 6:6-7). Paul elsewhere explains: when we have been crucified with Christ, we no longer live, but Christ lives in us. The life we now live in the body, we live by faith in the Son of God, who loved and gave himself for us (cf. Gal. 2:20).

In Romans, chapter 7, the Apostle writes: "when we were controlled by the sinful nature, the sinful passions aroused by the law were at work in our bodies, so that we bore fruit for death" (v. 5). He further declares the Law becomes the instrument of indictment (vv. 7-24). Paul had said knowledge of sin came through the Law (3:20). This refers to sin in particular, and the Law plumbs the depth of mankind's revolt against God. The Apostle states: "The law was added so that the trespass might increase" (5:20). That is, God gave the Mosaic law to make mankind aware of their sinfulness (cf. 7:5; Gal. 3:19).

The apostle Paul continues: "the law is holy, and the commandment is holy, righteous and good" (Rom, 7:12). The Law sets forth what the nature of a person ought to be and proclaims the moral precepts universally relevant to human happiness. Since holy law kindles revolt, a person appears depraved, living only after the flesh. Romans, chapter 7, asserts law does much more than focus and intensify mankind's guilt, or actual wrongdoing (vv. 9-11, 13). It also exposes a depraved nature behind the individual infractions. Paul gives the key: "So now, no longer am I the one doing it, but sin which indwells me. For I know that nothing good dwells in me, that is in my flesh . . . " (vv. 17-18, NASB).

Not only our sins need to be dealt with, but also the nature of sin that prompts the self-life in all its bold assertions. Our idol-self would crucify Christ's Spirit within us that it might live on. We might translate Paul's cry (Rom. 7:24) to declare, "O wretched self that I am! Who shall deliver me from this body of death, this living death which is the self?"[13]

The moral concept of flesh as mankind under the rule of sin is the crucial issue. Sin must be put to death in the flesh. "For what the law was powerless to do in that it was weakened by the sinful nature, God did by sending his own Son in the likeness of sinful man to be a sin offering. And so he condemned sin in sinful man, . . . " (Rom. 8:3).

Salvation From Sin Now

Richard Baxter, in his book, *The Saints Everlasting Rest*, said: "Despair of ever being saved, 'except thou be born again;' or of 'seeing God without holiness;' or of having part in Christ, except thou 'love him above father, mother, or thy own life.' "[14]

Such anguish becomes one of the first steps to heaven. There is no reserve of innate goodness from which to draw. Our only hope is by faith in God's grace, through the crucified and risen Savior. Without Christ we become lost sinners in despair. But with Him, we have a glorious hope of forgiveness and eternal life. "For Christ's love compels us, because we are convinced that one died for all, and therefore all died. And he died that all those who live should no longer live for themselves, but for him who died for them, and was raised again" (2 Cor. 5:14-15).

The guilty may be transformed from a life of sinning—here and now—in the flesh. Coming to Jesus in faith, the seeker finds forgiveness and a new way of life. It is not as though we can only receive God's salvation by leaving our mortal bodies. We are not delivered from depravity in death. We limit God if we say pardon cannot be obtained and impurity cannot be removed while we live in the body. Holiness of heart and life, becoming like Christ, is His plan for all believers.

Christ suffered death on Calvary for both our justification and sanctification. God receives us, as we by faith confess with profound gratitude, "Jesus died for me!" But we must also see ourselves dying there. Of Jesus, Paul declared, "The death he died, he died to sin once for all; but the life he lives, he lives to God. In the same way, count yourselves dead to sin but alive to God in Christ Jesus" (Rom. 6:10-11).

Rescue from the penalty of sin meant Jesus' death for me, so freedom from the tyranny of sinful self requires my death with Him. By faith we understand Christ's death brought not only an at-one-ment for sin, but a triumph over all sin. We become transformed to stand before God as fully redeemed human beings. The curse of sin is canceled and Satan is a defeated foe.

A correct doctrine of original sin becomes molded by several observations. First, flesh per se is not sinful. God sent His son, Jesus Christ, in the flesh, a human body, but He was not sinful. Second, the term "sinful flesh" depicts human nature infected by sin. This weakness has plagued every human being as a member of a fallen race under the domination of sin. Third, Christ came to provide forgiveness of actual sin, making obedience possible. The very root of mankind's rebellion became condemned because Jesus came in human flesh and always did the Father's will.

Christ reproved sin in the flesh that "the righteous requirements of the law might be fully met in us, who do not live according to our sinful nature but according to the Spirit" (Rom. 8:4). The power of God's indwelling Spirit enables us to crucify ourselves with Christ. The same Spirit prompts us to yield ourselves to the Divine will. Paul says, "Through Christ Jesus the law of the Spirit of life set me free from the law of sin and death" (v. 2).

The Apostle concludes that although mankind's depraved disposition stands under indictment, a holy, righteous nature becomes available through Christ. It remains a faith choice. The depraved and holy natures are compared in Romans 8:5-8:

> Those who live according to the sinful nature have their minds set on what that nature desires; but those who live in accordance with the Spirit have their minds set on what the Spirit desires. The mind of sinful man is death, but the mind controlled by the Spirit is life and peace, because the sinful mind is hostile to God. It does not submit to God's law, nor can it do so. Those controlled by the sinful nature cannot please God.

The contrast between the inborn self-bias "hostile to God" and life in the Spirit depicts mankind's way as opposed to God's way. Mankind will go on sinning so long as the bent to rebel remains. Christ gave himself for sin so a person's depraved nature might be cleansed. One becomes transformed by His Spirit to be a redeemed, holy, and obedient person.

The Savior bore our sins to bring us forgiveness. They were put under His feet, as it were, for our release. Our claim to "glorious freedom" from sin comes through His wondrous cross. That cross offers us new life in the fullness of God's grace, and it becomes the means of our spiritual progress for ever.

In *The Pilgrim's Progress*, John Bunyan writes how Christian leaves the City of Destruction and passes through the Wicket-gate. A burden remains on his back, weighing him down and making his travel hard. He soon comes to a hill "and upon that place stood a cross, and a little below, . . . a sepulchre. So I saw in my dream, that just as Christian came up with the Cross, his burden loosed from off his shoulders and fell from off his back, and began to tumble, and so continued . . . till it came to the mouth of the sepulchre, where it fell in, and I saw it no more.

"Then was Christian glad . . . and said with a merry heart, He hath given me rest by His sorrow, and life by His death. Then he stood still awhile to look and wonder; for it was very surprising to him that the sight of the Cross should thus ease him of his burden . . . . Now as he stood looking and weeping, behold, three Shining Ones came to him, and saluted him with 'Peace be to thee:' so the first said to him, 'Thy sins be forgiven thee' (Mark 2:5); the second stripped him of his rags, and clothed him with change of raiment; the third also set a mark on his forehead; and gave him a roll with a seal upon it (Zech. 3:4; Eph. 1:13), which he bid him look on as he ran, and that he should give it in at the celestial gate: So they went on their way. Then Christian gave three leaps for joy, and went on singing,

> "Thus far I did come laden with my sin;
> Nor could aught ease the grief that I was in,
> Till I came hither: what a place is this!
> Must here be the beginning of my bliss?
> Must here the burden fall from off my back?
> Must here the strings that bound it to me crack?
> Blessed cross! blessed sepulchre! blessed rather be
> The Man that there was put to shame for me!"[15]

Our sin is the kind of wrong that put Christ to death. Our pride, our blindness, our self-will, our self-seeking, our failure to respond to God's love and Word—all filled the hearts of those who tried and condemned Jesus. Through the shared guilt of mankind, you and I partake in the sin that crucified the Lord of glory.

Gazing upon that scene of anguish, we realize Jesus' forgiveness is the kind of pardon we need. He cries out from the Cross: "Father, forgive them, for they do not know what they are doing" (Luke 23:34a). It is no cheap forgiveness—no cut-rate grace. Christ places himself beside us, pleading for our pardon though He paid with His life. The Cross is the symbol of the great price God gave to forgive the sin of mankind.

Jesus' forgiving grace precedes any action on our part to seek pardon. This great reaching love of God has suffered throughout the ages because of mankind's selfish folly. But divine forgiveness meets a person in any station to bestow pardon. God shows His love for us: "While we were still sinners, Christ died for us" (Rom. 5:8).

Divine forgiveness is a profound mystery. Bishop Angus Dun explores its depths, dealing with the Seven Last words of Jesus. In his book, *The King's Cross*, Dun says:

> "In Christ upon the cross, we see the love of God and love for sinners dwelling in one heart. His love of God does not hold him back from loving sinners. His love of sinners does not stand in the way of his love of God. God and sinners can meet in his heart. They are not, then, hopelessly separated. The life that can take two alienated lives within itself is a reconciling life. Christ's is a reconciling life.
>
> "The forgiveness of Christ came to men with such authority as being the forgiveness of God, because men recognized that he who loved them was the same One who judged them with the stern judgment of God. He did not depart from God in drawing near to them. Therefore they could come near to God in drawing near to him.
>
> "The deepest agony in Christ's passion was the pain of giving such forgiveness. To love purity and love adulterers, to love kindness and love the unkind, to love generosity and love the covetous, to love God and love sinners, that is the inmost secret of Calvary."[16]

Seeing a perfect love for God and a perfect love for sinners dwelling in one heart, we become drawn to the Cross. The Word of the Cross says, "Son, your sins are forgiven" (Mark 2:5). The holy sacrament of the Cross proclaims: "This is my blood of the covenant, which is poured out for many for the forgiveness of sins" (Matt. 26:28). We may thus believe the Word, gladly receive the pledge, and freely taste the joy of sins forgiven.

Every child of Adam's race may be reborn in Christ. By faith in Him, any person may confess his need, turn from the practice of sin, and live in righteousness. The power of this new birth repels the temptation to sin. The old sinful habits become broken, freeing believers from their fatal grip. We stand released through divine grace and pardon. Forgiveness comes as we confess and repent of our sins.

The Spirit of Christ abides to empower and purify, moving to depose our rebellious selfish nature. The happy believer receives a grand exchange—a disposition to do God's will. As Adam reproduced sinful children in the flesh, Christ brings forth children in the Spirit unto true holiness to be like Him.

The Lord's perfect sacrifice for all of mankind's sin spikes the indictment of the Scripture against the entire race. Our deadly suspicion of God can never be altered apart from Christ's atonement. We stand accused, condemned until our faith reaches out to the salvation God so freely offers through the Savior.

Charles Wesley raises hope and joy to ruined and perplexed peoples—both of 18th century England and of our day. His hymn, "O for a Thousand Tongues," proclaims a message of forgiveness and release that expects a ready response:

> 1. O for a thousand tongues to sing
>   My great Redeemer's praise;
>   The glories of my God and King,
>   The triumphs of his grace!
>
> 3. Jesus! the name that charms our fears,
>   That bids our sorrows cease;
>   'Tis music in the sinner's ears,
>   'Tis life, and health, and peace.
>
> 4. He breaks the power of canceled sin,
>   He sets the prisoner free;
>   His blood can make the foulest clean;
>   His blood availed for me.
>
> 6. Hear him, ye deaf; his praise, ye dumb,
>   Your loosened tongues employ;
>   Ye blind, behold your Savior come;
>   And leap, ye lame, for joy.[17]

God's solemn indictment of sin becomes tempered in His mercy and grace. The glory of His salvation calls for our response of faith. His gracious gift may be received or ignored. To reject the holy kiss of forgiveness through Christ is to spurn eternal life. What a difference accepting the power of divine love makes in our lives!

NOTES

1. A. B. Davidson, *The Theology of the Old Testament* (New York: Charles Scribner's Sons, 1917), 210-211.

2. Cf. Donald Metz, *Studies in Biblical Holiness* (Kansas City: Beacon Hill Press, 1971), 64-70.

3. Cited in Ibid., 67.

4. Cited in Ibid., 68.

5. Cited in Ibid., 67.

6. H. Orton Wiley, *Christian Theology* (Kansas City: Beacon Hill Press, 1953), II, 99.

7. Thomas N. Ralston, *Elements of Divinity*, 131.

8. H. Orton Wiley, *Christian Theology*, II, 100.

9. Henry E. Brockett, *The Christian and Romans 7* (Kansas City: Beacon Hill Press, 1972), 17.

10. Ibid., 26.

11. Richard E. Howard, *Newness of Life* (Kansas City: Beacon Hill Press, 1975), 39-40.

12. Milton S. Agnew, *More than Conquerors* (Chicago: Salvation Army, 1959), 57.

13. Dwight Hervey Small, *The High Cost of Holy Living*, 64.

14. Richard Baxter, *The Saints' Everlasting Rest* (New York: American Tract Society, n.d.), 132.

15. John Bunyan, *The Pilgrim's Progress* (New York: Books, Inc., 1946), 36-37.

16. Cited in F. W. Dillistone, *Jesus Christ and His Cross* (Philadelphia: The Westminster Press, 1953), 133-134.

17. *Hymnal of the Methodist Episcopal Church*, 1.

CHAPTER IV

Redeemed from Sin unto Righteousness

Count Leo Tolstoy, noted 19th century Russian writer, tells of his conversion, how he turned from evil to good. He said: "Five years ago faith came to me. I believed in the doctrine of Jesus, and all my life was suddenly changed. I ceased to desire that which previously I had desired, and on the other hand, I took to desiring what I had never desired before. That which formerly used to appear good in my eyes appeared evil, and that which used to appear evil appeared good."[1]

Our redemption from a life of sin to doing good comes because of Christ's complete sacrifice. All attempts to find lasting hope apart from Him become futile. But so far as God's saving power reaching any person, there remain no hopeless cases.

Charles Wesley responds to the Divine provision to redeem mankind from sin in his hymn, "Abba, Father"—Romans 8:15:[2]

> Arise, my soul, arise;
> Shake off thy guilty fears;
> The bleeding Sacrifice
> In my behalf appears:
> Before the throne my Surety stands,
> My name is written on His hands.

Mankind's life with God was to be an endless hope, but in parting from Him it became a hopeless end. Turning from God, mankind began a daring venture that soon fell into ruin. Their treason against God left life useless, though they exalted themselves and acted in self-will.

God's first law to Adam required obedience. It was a simple decree; a person had nothing to inquire after or to dispute. He had only to obey his Creator and Benefactor. The basic divine attribute revealed was holiness: "Be holy, because I am holy" (1 Pet. 1:16; cf. Lev. 11:44-45).

Holiness in God, His right and just actions and attitudes set our duty to seek His righteousness. As all sin stems from self-will, all virtues spring from obedience and submission to God. His commandments, especially the Decalogue, call mankind to do that holy will. Our holiness is to be like God's even though His is original and absolute, and ours is in "clay vessels," fashioned by the Holy Spirit.

Since it seemed impossible to keep the Law, people have thought it was their enemy. The apostle Paul became inspired to call the Law a "schoolmaster" (KJV), pointing to righteousness and holiness (Gal. 3:24). Whereas Adam broke God's law, Christ, the second Adam, came to fulfill it.

Mankind's debased state did not slam the door shut against God's saving action. The divine Son became born in human flesh to reveal God's holy love to us sinners, meeting our helpless need with mercy and undeserved favor. Jesus Christ came to reveal divine salvation to sinners by dying for them. His willing sacrifice declares God's holiness, the fatal evil of sin, the triumph of divine love, and His grace ordains new life.

Think of a tuning fork to hear and grasp God's divine revelation as redemption. God struck the world with Christ's atoning act. The sound clearly rang out in the apostles' word of reconciliation, and it reverberates throughout New Testament Scripture.[3] Those true gospel tones still ring out to this day, heard by all who will listen.

Our guilt becomes exposed at the Cross by God's judgement and mercy. Yet, in Jesus' life-sacrifice, our sin becomes cancelled by forgiveness and cleansing. Our faith in Him removes condemnation, and our doubts become erased. Joyful trust claims the safety that goes unseen by the impenitent's dulled vision. God deals with our sin through Christ as the One who eternally and lovingly knows us.

Many Christians have supposed that despite a person's redemption, he remains an unchecked sinner. One's condition is thought so ruined that divine acceptance occurs only because of Christ's miraculous cover. The endlessly sinning Christian seeks credit under the righteousness of his Lord. Does this mean we continue doing daily the same sins, without improvement, and no promise of deliverance in Christ?

No! We stand called to answer God's redemption in Jesus Christ by our obedience of faith. Christ becomes revealed as our deliverer to lead us in righteousness and holiness. He becomes our power and adequacy for cleansing from sin and the conquest to live a holy life. He enables us to have victory over the reign of sin in our lives.

When our faith takes hold God does not prove himself to us. Rather, it's like "He comes home." We became created by and for Him. His presence brings the glad and gracious knowledge that He has forgiven us. Conscious of God's loving pardon, we find peace and rest that goes beyond our understanding.[4]

But our concept of justification by faith should not exclude the doctrine of the living Christ or the work of the Holy Spirit. God wants to bring our wills and consciences into harmony with His moral universe. Because He created all things, He stands able to redeem all things unto himself (Col. 1:15-18). The ground of our faith is one with the object of it—God in Christ reconciling the world to himself. Jesus Christ is our authority in all personal and social affairs. He leads us in obedience and redeems us from moral death. Sin's curse becomes broken, as Christ releases us from its deadly sting.

Christ himself fully met the holy law, which we can break but never depose. From the vantage point of the Cross, Christ became raised to reign over sin and death and hell. Through the power of His Holy Spirit, Jesus restores to us the life we have wasted and lost the vigor to regain.

Mankind's Sin Judged

Our world ignores the trouble caused by its sins. It merely regards them as adventures in experience. Should painful consequences attend such affairs, most people attach no guilt.

William Gladstone, famed British statesman of the 19th century, was once asked: "What is the chief want in the modern world?"

Gladstone quickly replied: "The sense of sin." His answer speaks to an ongoing lack in mankind.

Sin is a revelation fact—not a common-sense fact. The Bible says there is something profoundly wrong at the base of things. But no natural human becomes bothered about sin unless he becomes convicted by the Holy Spirit. Of the Spirit, Jesus said: "When he comes, he will convict the world of guilt in regard to sin and righteousness and judgment: in regard to sin, because men do no believe in me; in regard to righteousness, because I am going to the Father, . . . and in regard to judgment, because the prince of this world now stands condemned" (John 16:8-9).

Sins become offenses against the Divine law of love, the law of Christ. John sums it up precisely when he wrote: "And this is his command: to believe in the name of his Son, Jesus Christ, and to love one another as he commanded us" (1 John 3:23).

Sinners remain oblivious to their peril. Unless we love God we stand condemned to death. We find it easy to ignore the repugnance of sin and the stranglehold of its curse. We tend to define sin to suit our own selfish whims, and rationalize any wrongness to seem alright. We easily lapse into increasing cycles of evil conduct.

However, sin is not our failure to live up to some ideal we have raised for ourselves. Neither is it simply transgressing the law of a city or state. Against the backdrop of eternity, sin becomes rebellion against a righteous, holy God. When we disobey God a chasm becomes dredged between Him and us that we cannot bridge. We are as aliens from our loving Father.

Guilt surrounds sin like a pall. Though evil is a static concept, sin occurs as personal disobedience to God for which we become responsible.

David beseeched God, "Against you, you only, have I sinned and done what is evil in your sight, . . . " (Psa. 51:4). God's holiness reproves sin with guilt and makes it personal, pricking the conscience.

Our sin becomes defined not so much by law as by a Person, the Lord Jesus Christ. His holy life in contrast with the lives of sinners asserts a shocking and shameful verdict. When Jesus called the fishermen to be disciples, Simon Peter fell at Jesus' knees and cried, "Go away from me, Lord; I am a sinful man!" (luke 5:8). Christ's coming not only reveals the righteous holiness and love of God, but the wickedness of mankind.

Even at birth we become estranged from God. As a race we have forfeited the good and holy relationship for which He made us. That bond became shattered by disobedience. We cannot, of ourselves, break the impact of disgrace and appeal to God's grace. Our salvation depends on His love, mercy, and grace that goes before any futile human attempts.

Each of us becomes defeated by sin. As the prophet said, "We all, like sheep, have gone astray, each of us has turned to his own way; . . . " (Isa. 53:6). When the Holy Spirit confronts us with this truth, every person is compelled to say, "This means me."

Sin is mankind's declaration of independence from God. It has been so from the beginning. Paul declared, "For all have sinned and fall short of the glory of God" (Rom. 3:23). Scripture depicts mankind as a ruin of what God made him to be. In each of us, broken fragments remain of that first holy creation, evidence of the magnificent creature God made in His own image.

Our personal human powers have often presumed a wondrous promise of what we might become. But any promise awaits divine redemption. Without God's saving grace, mankind's plight is a dead-end. We become bound by the grievous habits of sin and the curse of death.

King Mezentius, of the Etruscans, a country beyond the Tiber River, became banished by his subjects. He practiced a vile torment against his enemies. He sought vengeance by binding a dead body to a condemned person, face to face, hand to hand, foot to foot, leaving the wretched victim to await death in that loathsome embrace.

The Apostle may refer to that living death when, speaking of sin, he said, "O wretched man that I am! who shall deliver me from the body of this death?" (Rom. 7:24, KJV). Whether Paul knew of Mezentius or not, he rightly described the deadly curse and power of sin that plagues all humanity. Paul answers his own question of rescue from sin's death. He says, "Thanks be to God through Jesus Christ our Lord!" (Rom. 7:25). He claimed Christ came to release sin's captives from that evil bondage, and to provide triumph over death.

History records how mankind has twisted life on earth into chaos. By nature, we join the human race as objects of divine wrath (Eph. 2:3). Our revolt against God pampers the cravings of our sinful nature in pursuit of its desires and thoughts. Though God's moral purity condemns sin to death, His holy love provides our redemption.

Christian truth proclaims life is founded on the primacy of Jesus and the finality of virtue. But world civilizations ever gloss over the tumult and wrath incurred by sin. People exalt the progress of technology, and are blind to their need of divine pardon. Nominal Christians have presumed the goodness of God without caring to obey His righteous commands. They seek the paradise lost by that first sinful pair, trying to secure it without the forgiveness of the Lord God.

Earthly misery and woe extend from earliest human history. Since sin and judgment afflict countless millions, one wonders that God created man in the first place. Even so, when all of God's dealings and exploits are fit together, we find His ways are just and perfect. The Judge of all the earth has always done wisely and right. We can trust Him though we cannot trace Him, and believe where we do not understand Him.

Yet tragic fate follows the human race from that first disobedience. Sin's pollution degrades all mankind, reaching unborn generations. For instance, babies born of mothers who smoke cigarettes, or use drugs, or drink alcoholic beverages, have affected lives healthwise. Sin expresses itself in guilt as it strikes home to us individually. We can only cling to God's forgiveness and reconciliation through Christ's cross.

We dare not minimize sin. It stands as an affront to God's perfect holiness—a threat to our race and to our very lives. Our sin becomes more serious than symbols of straying sheep or wandering prodigals—we become doomed rebels. In willful revolt we struggle with bloody weapons in our hands. Unless we confess and repent, God's forgiveness cannot be applied to bring us "newness of life."

How may we be brought to a proper sense of sin-guilt? Isaiah's vision of God's holiness revealed the prophet's own iniquity (Isaiah 6). Divine truth still proclaims the pure holiness of God to all who will hear. His very nature prevents Him from condoning any sin. Rather, by the gracious gift of His Son, dying on the Cross, sin faces judgment and sinners become redeemed.

God in holy love must judge sin—not waive it. His judgment of sin becomes burning wrath—the obverse side of holy love. Our call unto holiness is not to mystical absorption into the being of God, but to a concrete righteous life made like His, cleansed and sustained at white heat. "For our God is a consuming fire" (Heb. 12:29). The prophet Malachi said the Lord is like "a refiner's fire," fire which purifies the precious metal (chap. 3).

Those who deplore any thought that God should be angry with us as sinners should think what that implies. If God cares enough about us to be angry with us in our sins, He also cares enough to redeem us from its curse. Only such divine love could act to save lost humanity.

After being locked up for months in a Nazi prison, Pastor Martin Niemoller emerged and said, "It took me a long time to learn that God is not the enemy of His enemies!"[5]

God Forgives Confessed Sin

God freely offers our fallen race redemption, a solution of the sin question in each person's case. Certainly, any so-called remedy that allows for remaining sin cannot be what God plans to bestow. "His plan is never to save a man in his sins, but to save him from his sins."[6] Joseph and Mary received such a divine promise for humanity when the angel told Mary she was to be the mother of a mighty Savior. "You are to give him the name, Jesus, because he will save his people from their sins" (Matt. 1:21).

A salvation that really saves must transform the sinner's moral and physical life. It must make a person enough like God that he can live free from sinful rebellion here and be fit to dwell with Him in heaven. Anything less than this would render God's plan a sham. We must like what God likes, hate what He hates, seeking His holy presence forever. It becomes absurd to think anyone with sin ruling his being would relish the Divine presence.

Whatever sin we confess to God, He forgives (1 John 1:9). To confess literally means to say the same thing God says about our sin. This must join true repentance, a forsaking of and a godly sorrow for our sins. God doesn't pardon our lame excuses. Our place of confession is the point of forgiveness. God pledges to meet us here. Throughout humanity's wayward history, nothing stands more striking than God's readiness to forgive. His great grace grants us pardon—it is not by our worthiness, or that we somehow earn pardon by doing good works. He faithfully moves to restore the penitent to His loving favor.

Believers become drawn to cast themselves on the merits of Jesus Christ. Atonement must be claimed in His shed blood. Trusting in the Divine promises, believers find the total cure for their sin. A miracle occurs. A person becomes aware that he has been justified from all his sins, before the Judge of all earth. The righteous Judge forgives, and one's transgressions become blotted out of the Lord's memory and of heaven's record.

In Christian experience, repentance and regeneration, conversion and forgiveness, justification and sanctification, proceed as one walks in God's truth. Our spiritual relationship with God contains both the elements of an instantaneous event and a continuous process. Paul views the Divine justifying act as beginning the sanctification of the sinner. Born again of the Holy Spirit, one is launched upon a holy life that acts and thinks according to God's love (cf. Romans 5).

Our new spiritual status bears fruit in daily miracles. When God forgives, He sets no limits. He blots out every sin from our record. The Psalmist assures us, "As far as the east is from the west, so far has he removed our transgressions from us" (Psa. 103:12). Then when we identify ourselves with Christ, we become "changed into the same image from glory to glory, even as by the Spirit of the Lord" (2 Cor. 3:18, KJV).

Where once the shadows of sin prevailed in human lives, now shines the steady light of holiness.[7] That light reveals the reality of newfound hope through Jesus Christ. Where once an ever-deepening despair had settled, now rises the victor's cry, "I can do all things through Him who strengthens me" (Phil. 4:13, NASB).

This truth sustains us amid the harsh realities of life, meeting the wrongs we have done and the hurtful things we have experienced. Forgiveness works day by day, creating goodness in the forgiven by its own inherent power and love. A person who has realized forgiveness knows that pardon itself, not his own effort, is the true moral power that secures his future.

When Christ's salvation quickens one's heart, the believer develops an appetite for righteousness and begins obedient service. Jesus said, "Blessed are those who hunger and thirst for righteousness, for they will be filled" (Matt. 5:6). A salvation that doesn't result in such service becomes spurious. God acted in loving purpose to redeem the human race. Christians in turn reach out in love for the lost, wayward people, or their own salvation becomes threatened.

The Bible reveals God's wondrous and faithful dealings with mankind. His Holy Spirit inspires and applies the Word to all who will listen. The Lord says through the prophet: " . . . my word that goes out from my mouth: It will not return to me empty, but will accomplish what I desire and achieve the purpose for which I sent it" (Isa. 55:11).

The Psalmist declared, "Your word is a lamp to my feet and a light to my path" (119:105). God's Word proclaims His will and way, and convicts us of sin, prompting us to accept His truth. The Holy Spirit uses the prodding Word, urging to salvation, even making young children aware of their need of forgiveness.

Penitent sinners do not remain as fugitives from the vengeance of broken laws, nor are they saddled with unrighteousness. We may enjoy God's pardon—cleared before the holy court of heaven. The Lord God says, "I will forgive their wickedness, and will remember their sins no more" (Heb. 8:12). It is all made possible because of Christ's better covenant, the power of His blood.

Martin Luther, while a monk, had a vision of Satan one night in his cell. Satan appeared before him as the tempter with great rolls, and bade Luther to read. He saw in his dream that these contained the record of his own life, and they were written in his own hand. The tempter said to him, "Is that true, did you write it?"

Luther could only confess it was all true. Scroll after scroll became unrolled, and these wrung the same admission from him. Satan, the evil one, prepared to depart, after dashing the monk's hopes to the depths of despair. Then, like a flash, it came to Luther in his vision that on which his salvation rested. He quickly turned to the tempter and declared, "It is true, every word of it, but write across it all: 'The blood of Jesus Christ, God's Son, cleanseth from all sin.' "[8]

The cleansing power of Jesus' blood, applied by God's Holy Spirit, ever transforms believers to new life. Old things pass away—all things become new. A creating God can not be content with any ruin of sin.

A New Life

Forgiveness of sin transforms the believer's heart and mind, changing, raising that person to a higher level of relationship with God. A new Christ-nature becomes imparted, giving spiritual life to all who receive it. When the first pair sinned, they died spiritually, and eventually perished physically. From that day, every child of Adam's race has entered this life with the curse of sin upon him.

Christ's atonement covers us during infancy, cleansing our unknown sin by prevenient grace. But when one reaches the age of accountability and chooses the way of sin, spiritual death befalls that person. The age of accountability occurs when a child becomes aware of the difference between right and wrong. All the days of a sinner become spent in a death that separates from God's life.

The New Testament calls us to the Cross, Jesus' place of death, to receive new life. This purpose filled the mind of Jesus Christ. The apostle

Paul declared, "Christ died for our sins according to the Scriptures, . . . " (1 Cor. 15:3). Though the birth of Jesus Christ is basic to our salvation, the Cross and not the cradle exudes saving power. The Lord Jesus died that we might find the fullness of life.

But the Cross should not be viewed as a mere life-saving device for one's own personal escape. Nor was it simply an exhibition of divine love. The Cross became God's act in Christ that worked the redemption of our fallen race. There, God intervened as the Savior of the world—because of His boundless holy love. He honored His own character at the supreme cost of His own sacrifice.

On the other hand, Jesus became crucified as mankind's representative, confessing God's holiness and justice while bearing sin's judgment. His sacrifice reconciled guilty mankind to holy God. P. T. Forsyth declares, "A holy God self-atoned in Christ is the moral center of the sinful world. Our justification has its key in God's justification of himself."[9]

Dietrich Bonhoeffer, Lutheran churchman martyred by the Nazis, said such divine grace "is costly because it costs a man his life, and it is grace because it gives a man the only true life. It is costly because it condemns sin, and it is grace because it justifies the sinner."[10]

The cross of Christ posted divine reconciliation in history and bridged the way for God's kingdom. It stood as the pledge of that kingdom yet to be consummated in the age to come. Our earth is not big enough to contain the whole of God's final redemption. This suggests another reason why there must be "a new heaven and a new earth" (Rev. 21:1).

When we confess our need to God and plead the atonement of His Son, we receive His pardon of sins and gain everlasting life. The Spirit often appeals with a keen sense of need. The tender minds of small children may be led to a saving knowledge of the Lord Jesus. All persons must respond in childlike faith to receive the forgiveness of God and acceptance through our Lord Jesus Christ. Divine forgiveness need not be understood—only accepted! The psalmist David said, "Such knowledge is too wonderful for me, too lofty for me to attain" (139:6).

This new spiritual life compares to what Adam and Eve lost in the Garden of Eden. The life of fellowship they forfeited becomes restored to each penitent heart. A person, once dead in trespasses and sins, becomes alive unto God. Every repenting believer lives again with the life of God. We call this regeneration, being born again by the Holy Spirit.

No one may see the kingdom that Jesus founded without this "new birth." It becomes a spiritual transaction that prompts a change in physical action. We are "called out" from a life of sin, unto righteousness, to join the body of Christ. His body, the Church, represents Him here on earth, being members of an invisible union.

Discipleship is the necessary corollary of receiving divine grace. As Bonhoeffer put it, "The only man who has the right to say that he is justified by grace is the man who has left all to follow Christ."[11] This experience of justification and new life is signaled by "the witness of the Spirit." Paul declares, "The Spirit himself testifies with our spirit that we are God's children" (Rom. 8:16). An inner consciousness bears witness that God approves our sincere remorse on the merits of His Son's atonement. Through our faith in Him, we become forgiven to live anew.

When we abandon ourselves to God's mercy and grace in repentance and faith, His Spirit gives us witness. The Holy Spirit grants the surety of divine pardon, for God never mocks His obedient children. If we doubt His work in us, something lacks in our surrender or in our faith. Our blessed assurance requires full assent to make wrongs right. God accepts our desire to make restitution of past sins and offenses, and forgives us. Then the Holy Spirit enables us to obey His leadership, making such apologies, returning stolen things, and correcting all wrongs possible.

Divine forgiveness opens the door to a new and wonderful life. When the burdens of sin and guilt become removed from our hearts and minds, we become freed to live anew. Scripture reveals that when Jesus forgave people, their lives at once gained new meaning and purpose.

Joy wells up in the hearts of those who have been brought from darkness to light. That fountain of joy washes away the burden of sins that had been dragging transgressors toward hell. The sense of forgiveness compels a loving response for God the Father, Son, and Holy Spirit. Calvary takes on a hallowed meaning, and daily fellowship with God becomes very real.

Every born again person should testify of God's saving power. Our Lord declared, "Whoever acknowledges me before men, I will also acknowledge him before my Father in heaven" (Matt. 10:32). The apostle Paul further states, "For it is with your heart that you believe and are justified, and it is with your mouth that you confess and are saved" (Rom. 10:10).

To be forgiven becomes a peerless experience. Some of the most lyrical outbursts of poetry and praise, both in the Old and New Testaments, are those that celebrate forgiveness. The prophet Micah offers a pertinent question and answer. He says: "Who is a God like you, who pardons sin and forgives the transgression of the remnant of his inheritance? You do not stay angry forever but delight to show mercy" (7:18).

God's mercy and pardon are His crowning glory. Samuel Davies penned his amazement in this verse:[12]

> Great God of wonders! all Thy ways
> Are worthy of Thyself—Divine;
> But the bright glories of Thy grace
> Beyond Thine other wonders shine.
> Who is a pardoning God like Thee,
> Or who has grace so rich and free?

The word of the Lord is: ". . . whoever comes to me I will never drive away" (John 6:37). God persists to confront people and nations and cultures in judgment and mercy. He offers eternal life to us through the sacrifice of Jesus Christ. In the light of the crucified and risen Savior, the disciples declared, "This is the Lord: we have waited for him, and he will save us" (cf. Isa. 25:9).

Christ's cross is not simply a sign of death and defeat—it is a symbol of victory—both His and ours. His crucifixion both fulfilled God's salvation plan and became the means of new life for believers. Jesus' sacrificial act of atonement by the shedding of His blood on Calvary is the sinner's only plea. There is no other way to find peace with God.

Theologians have approached Christ's work from three aspects—the Cross as triumph, as satisfaction, and as regeneration. No single view supplies the full meaning. God's saving grace should not be thought of as only procured by Christ's atonement. Neither should the Lord Jesus be imagined as offering an equivalent for our punishment in sin. Nor is guilt transferred as if it were a debit that could be canceled by divine finance.[13]

In 2 Cor. 5:14—6:2, Paul describes the end of Christ's work as "reconciliation," and its meaning as atonement. The apostle says, "God was reconciling the world to himself in Christ, not counting men's sins against them . . . God made him who had no sin to be sin for us, so that in him we might become the righteousness of God" (5:19, 21).

We may rightly define "atonement" as the covering of sin by something that God himself provided. Sin is thus covered by God through the shedding of blood and sacrifice of His Son. "Reconciliation" becomes the total result of Christ's work in changing the relation between God and mankind from hostility to peace.[14]

Also at issue is the perfect holiness of God—His moral majesty and His absolute goodness. Christians sometimes lose touch with the Lord God of the Bible, whose majesty is a His mercy. They construe His love in solely sentimental ways. This wrongly views divine forgiveness as indulgence.

The essence of God's love is its awful purity. Divine virtue cannot traffic with sin—all sin must be judged. Yet God is the holy Father who loves all His children with a seeking love throughout the ages. This self-giving love, that desires nothing but our loving response, deals of necessity with human acts of sin and the sinful human nature. Love stands relentless against evil.

The penitent sinner must have a certain state of mind to exercise faith that saves. He must have a godly sorrow to forsake the practice of sinning. The Christian believer seeking heart purity, before he can fully trust, must also reach a certain state. One comes to a sense of nothingness without the indwelling Spirit. That person becomes moved to consecrate his entire being to be used of God, according to His will.

On the one hand, we see the sin of mankind—on the other, the holiness of God. How is mankind to be reconciled to God? As sinners, we cannot of ourselves atone. Martin Luther observed that if we could, we would be "the proudest jackasses under heaven."[15]

A divine miracle has happened to right the wrongness between God and mankind. That act has redressed God's holiness to alter the estranged relationship between them. It offers repair to broken fellowship, and restores the severed communion. God himself acted to bring us new life through His Son's death on the Cross.

Charles Wesley voices this hope in "Alive in Christ:"[16]

> 1. And can it be that I should gain
> An int'rest in the Savior's blood?
> Died he for me, who caused his pain?
> For me, who him to death pursued?
> Amazing love! How can it be
> That thou, my God, shouldst die for me?

Jesus Christ brings freedom from the guilt and power of sin. The person who once was a slave to sin is by faith made "Christ's free man." When the Lord Jesus enters a life, peace comes. Those who remain in their sins have no peace. Their hearts become condemned by conscience, memory, and logic. They despair that they can ever know peace. But when any person allows Christ entrance, forgiveness comes, and with it, peace.

One can truly join Wesley's hymn, saying:

> 5. No condemnation now I dread;
> Jesus, and all in him, is mine;
> Alive in him, my living Head,
> And clothed in righteousness divine,
> Bold I approach the eternal throne
> And claim the crown through Christ, my own.

Every person must be born again through Christ. He only has the power to work such miracles in our lives. His indwelling Spirit is the secret of the new human creature. "Therefore, if anyone is in Christ, he is a new creation; the old is gone, the new has come!" (2 Cor. 5:17).

Remember, this new life remains costly.

NOTES

1. Paul Lee Tan, *Encyclopedia of 7700 Illustrations* (Rockville, Md.: Assurance Publishers, 1984), 1230.

2. *Hymnal of the Methodist Episcopal Church*, 266.

3. P. T. Forsyth, *The Gospel and Authority* (Minneapolis: Augsburg Publishing House, 1971), 85.

4. A. M. Hunter, *P. T. Forsyth* (Philadelphia: Westminster Press, 1974), 50.

5. Paul Lee Tan, *Encyclopedia of 7700 Illustrations*, 459.

6. J. G. Morrison, *Our Lost Estate* (Kansas City: Nazarene Publishing House, 1929), 41.

7. James S. Stewart, *A Man in Christ* (New York: Harper & Row, n.d.), 260.

8. A. Gordon Nasby (ed.), *1041 Sermon Illustrations, Ideas, and Expositions* (Grand Rapids: Baker Book House, 1976), 123.

9. P. T. Forsyth, *The Justified God* (Independent Press, 1957), 94.

10. Cited by Dwight Hervey Small, *The High Cost of Holy Living*, 11.

11. Ibid., 12.

12. Cited by James S. Stewart, *A Faith to Proclaim* (New York: Charles Scribner's Sons, 1953), 49.

13. A. M. Hunter, *P.T. Forsyth*, 60.

14. Ibid.

15. Cited in Ibid., 61.

16. *Hymnal of the Methodist Episcopal Church*, 255-256.

CHAPTER V

Christ's Holy Atonement

Evangelist Dwight L. Moody, preaching on salvation from sin, once declared: "I must die or get somebody to die for me. If the Bible doesn't teach that, it doesn't teach anything. And that is where the atonement of Jesus Christ comes in."[1]

God's act of holy love redeems us through His Son's self-giving sacrifice. This severe side of divine love demands more than human merit. It awaits a Savior's dying love to cry, "Forgive them!" The life-blood that flowed at Calvary atones for all our sin. It brings God's justice and mercy together to provide salvation for undeserving believers.

The divine Father's first concern for us is holiness, for us to be holy like Him. His charge to the Heaven-sent Redeemer assures us that such holiness has been made available. Only the Savior sent by the Father can make full atonement for our sin. God offers His only begotten Son, a sacrifice sent from His own heart, to restore us. Our atonement is made to Him by himself in His Son, to satisfy His holy nature and law. No third party could suffice to offer such a sacrifice.

The cross of Christ has a double character. It is both an act of God and a deed done in humanity. The holy God becomes revealed as self-atoned through the gift of His Son. Jesus freely laid down His life that mankind might live righteous before God. A loving Christ did not die just to appease an angry God. This would destroy the moral unity of the Godhead. "What Christ presented to God for his complete joy and satisfaction was a perfect racial obedience."[2]

Jesus, the Son, became faced with the task of bringing mankind, as sinners, back to God, the Father. The Savior must provide grounds to forgive mankind's sin, and make him holy as God is holy (cf. Lev. 11:45; 1 Pet. 1:15-16). Christ's innocent death bridged the chasm of sin, which severed man from God. As Moody implied, Jesus died for us that we might regain life from God.

Christ made peace with the Father on our behalf, and without our knowledge. As P. T. Forsyth said, "Doing this for us was the condition of doing anything with us."[3] Jesus' death on the cross made an atonement to God's holiness—He did for us what we could not do for ourselves. The all-seeing God covered mankind's sin with the offering of His holy Son. God in Christ made the atonement and gave it finished and complete to mankind.

Two moral principles are the pulse of what God did in Christ, proving His perfect holiness. They are obedience and judgment. In both the Old and New Testaments obedience is the truth of sacrifice. As the always obedient Son, Jesus presented to the Father a perfect racial obedience for divine glory and satisfaction.

God sent His Son to offer himself to shed His blood for sinners. Our Lord Jesus made a total sacrifice of His will, and He fulfilled the Father's will in everything He did. The holy Father did not merely require an equal penalty, as if He were a great Shylock demanding his "pound of flesh," but rather, His Son's obedience. Jesus said, "For I have come down from heaven not to do my will but to do the will of him who sent me" (John 6:38).

Because God is holy, He must truly deal with all of people's sin. The Cross shows the other moral principle involved in what God did is judgment. God's just judgment becomes displayed when Christ died for us. Paul said, "God made him who had no sin to be sin for us, so that in him we might become the righteousness of God" (2 Cor. 5:21).

As the believer's justification and sanctification, Christ redeems us from the doom of sins and from the rule of sin over our body and spirit. He frees us from the penalty of sins and from the power of sin. His salvation deals with both the actual corrupt fruit and the evil nature that produces it. Paul shows this distinction between sins (Rom. 1:16—5:11) and (the) sin (5:12—7:25).

We may specifically relate the first action to Christ's work for the believer, and the second to His work in the believer. The first also declares God's action in forgiving "sins," and the second, His action in delivering from "sin," that which is the root of sinning. This refers to justification and entire sanctification, respectively. Though God can forgive sins, He cannot forgive or tolerate sin. It must be removed—put to death.[4]

In Jesus' dual role as Son of God and Son of man, He knew sin as God does, and experienced its effects as mankind does. Sin carries a penalty and curse, and Christ coming, entered that region and suffering of condemned humanity. Both the agony in Gethsemane and the cry of dereliction from the Cross suggest a descent into the God-forsakenness of hell. Jesus traversed the dark valley of God's penalty on sin, taking our place.

Justified by His Cross

Jews and Romans alike, when the Christian faith became proclaimed to the public, confidently declared: "This religious system cannot stand because its words depend on a cross—the death of its own leader. Beliefs based on such an ending will never last." Yet we now see that that Cross forever marks divine genius in triumph over evil.

Christ's whole life and death did justice to God's pure holiness by owning it with a true holiness equal to the Father's. This made forgiveness of the world's sin possible, which could only be achieved by judgment. Jesus came and lived personally sinless, but He joined the race for better, for worse. His union with humanity was such that He shared in its corporate sin and submitted to God's judgment on it.

Though the sins of mankind, and their violent nation nailed Jesus to the cross, He did not die as a martyr. Christ died at the right time according to divine purpose. He laid down His life as a sacrifice to rescue sinners. Jesus said, "The reason my Father loves me is that I lay down my life—only to take it up again. No one takes it from me, but I lay it down of my own accord. I have authority to lay it down and authority to take it up again" (John 10:17-18).

Jesus served as our racial representative in His sacrifice. It was not by evil humanity taking Christ, but by His freely choosing to identify himself with sinful mankind. By so doing, Christ issued, on our behalf, through flames of judgment, a unitary assertion of God's pure holiness. Christ's atonement for mankind bears the healing fruit of the world's reconciliation to the Creator.

Jesus saved the human race, and each of us becomes redeemed in a social salvation. The world becomes reconciled in principle without all people repenting and putting their trust in Christ for time and eternity. The act of atonement is done—it is not a thing to do. The cross of Christ became the world's great day of judgment. Jesus said, " Now is the time for judgment on this world; . . . But I, when I am lifted up from the earth, will draw all men to myself" (John 12:31-32).

The Dore Gallery in London once displayed a picture with a foreground filled with people of every station in life. All were turned with imploring looks upon a distant figure. An artist had painted Jesus Christ wearing robes of dazzling white, and He stood bearing a cross. With a hand uplifted, He beckoned to the weary, broken-hearted ones to come to Him. It was an artist's concept of how Christ draws all people unto himself. This sinful world of sorrow and woe needs One who pities the penitent, and who has power to forgive and restore ruined lives.

No intrinsic value should be attached to the Cross itself. That would be idolatrous and sinful. We should worship the Christ who died on it. At the cross, Jesus bears the sins of all mankind. Dying there at awful suffering to himself, Christ takes away our guilt and blame, and our sins become atoned. That cross reveals to supposed "good" people that their goodness is not good enough to please God.

Standing before the Cross, no one dares speculate about how his own goodness looks to God. Rather, a person is at first cast down and condemned by his sin. One thrashes about in guilt and hopelessness. By faith believers thrill to the joyous revelation that Christ is their saving kinsman who justifies life!

Even today this world becomes judged. But the final judgment will come at the end of this age. We must actualize Jesus' sacrifice by faith and apply His perfect offering to our individual needs. Then we may become the persons He intends for us to be. Christ's once-and-for-all death offers us salvation now and throughout eternity.

Forsyth's "prospective view" of the Atonement declares our human holiness remains latent in Christ's who alone must create it. He becomes both the pledge of God's holy love to us and of our response to it by a complete change of will and life.[5] The living Lord extends His work in the new humanity, the "new self, created to be like God in true righteousness and holiness" (Eph. 4:24).

Communion with Christ depends on His reconciling action to cover all history and to enter each person's life through the Holy Spirit. Jesus presents, with His own holy obedience, the penitent love He creates in His people. The Father accepts not only Christ, but those who remain in Him and with Him. We come to see the Almighty's majesty as His mercy and grace. His power moves to forgive, redeem, and settle all believers in holy worship. The divine kingdom will forever flourish in the new heaven and new earth.

Christ's bequest to His followers became himself—not simply a truth. His gift was a faith that demands we worship Him as Lord of all. It was the Cross, when the full meaning dawned on mankind by the resurrection through the spirit. Rising from the dead, Jesus became the subject matter and not merely the master of gospel preaching. He became Lord indeed, perfecting life through death.

Jesus became the complete Savior only in the finished salvation. His disciples soon saw that all He was to them flowed from the Cross. Christ, who became sin for all mankind on the Cross, also became for them God reconciling the world to himself. Jesus took our place at Calvary, dying for our sin, taking away its guilt, and fulfilled the Scriptures.

Our salvation centers on Jesus Christ. He is our Lord, our God—He saves us from the bondage of sin and the curse of death. He becomes Christ and Lord of all by His cross. He is God by that in Him which redeems us. The exercise of personal faith claims total forgiveness and final redemption in the Lord Jesus Christ.

Indeed, this experience doesn't merely include forgiveness—it *is* forgiveness. Pardon becomes the core of our personal encounter with Christ. God's holy love forgives because of what Jesus did at Calvary. Only the redeemed Church, the Body of Christ that knows forgiveness, has the key to the Savior and the keys to His kingdom.[6]

We worship Christ as Savior, Forgiver, Redeemer, Creator, and Judge of all mankind. The Church holds Christ's deity by her knowledge of justifying faith. His abundant pardon annuls our sin. We become restored into communion with God by faith in His Son, Jesus Christ. Being united with Christ is to be joined with God. Christ is God, and we are redeemed in Christ, God truly redeems us by His grace.

Jesus not only died to affect mankind, but to provide their salvation. He came—not simply to move mankind's hearts—to accomplish God's will in their lives. Believers also work to reconcile people unto God, pointing them to His great saving act—the Cross. Christ's atoning cross is the key that opens salvation's door, to the very heart of God.

Forgiveness of sins, the justifying aspect of regeneration, occurs when one has been born again of the Holy Spirit. He leads the believer to walk in obedience with the Lord. This preserves the pardon and new life that justification before God brings.

Our regeneration comes with adoption into the family of God. Justification offers pardon of all one's sin's, showing God's mercy and favor toward the sinner. Christ's new life becomes planted in the penitent's heart by divine grace. When God sees a sinner repent, turn from sin, He, for Christ's sake, adopts that person as a legal member of His holy family. One becomes both born again of the Holy Spirit and adopted into God's household.

Though regeneration imparts a new Christlike life to the believer, that life at times flows full, and then ebbs. Jesus refers to this needy state when He says, "I am come that they might have life, and that they might have it more abundantly" (John 10:10, KJV). In that same Gospel, He speaks of a saved person having spiritual life in Him like "a spring of water welling up to eternal life" (4:14). Christ also says that with the coming of the Holy Spirit, a believer would have "streams of living water" flowing from within him (John 7:38). It is a cleansing stream that affects every aspect of our lives.

Forgiven and Cleansed by His Blood

A little boy, asked what forgiveness is, gave a tender answer: "It is the odor that flowers breathe when they are trampled upon."

Every regenerated person has divine life imparted to him. He becomes born again of the Holy Spirit. Yet this new life that transforms one's heart becomes opposed by the nature of sin present from birth. Those past habits of sin have been forgiven and forsaken, the human heart becomes a battleground between the rule of sin and God's guidance. The selfish nature of sin and the obedient love of the Holy Spirit war against each other. What one loves, the other hates.

A. W. Tozer once drew the contrast that within the citadel of a believer's heart there were two tenants and two places of dwelling. There is the Self and the Lord Jesus; there is a throne and a cross. Whoever sits on the throne settles who is on the cross. If Self is on the throne, Christ is on the cross; but if Christ is on the throne, Self is on the cross. We must decide which tenant will reign in our lives, and which must be crucified.[7]

The justified Christian can love God, but he soon finds that love to be imperfect, incomplete. He also received the gracious ability to refrain from sin. But the bent to sin remains in his heart, and he remains disposed to yield to temptation. One may return to sins from which Christ rescued him, and deny the new life imparted by the Holy Spirit.

Notice the contrast and cure the apostle Paul proclaims in his Epistle to the Romans:

> For in my inner being I delight in God's law; but I see another law at work in the members of my body, waging war against the law of my mind and making me a prisoner of the law of sin at work

within my members. What a wretched man I am! Who will rescue me from this body of death? Thanks be to God—through Jesus Christ our Lord!

So then, I myself in my mind am a slave to God's law, but in the sinful nature a slave to the law of sin.

Therefore, there is now no condemnation for those who are in Christ Jesus, because through Christ Jesus the law of the Spirit of life set me free from the law of sin and death. For what the law was powerless to do in that it was weakened by the sinful nature, God did by sending his own Son to be a sin offering. (7:22—8:3).

This warfare in the reborn Christian's life does not so much involve conflict against outside foes as against the inner, native principle of sin. The old sinful nature of selfishness vies to put Self over God. Such rebellion has been at the root of every wilful sin from the beginning. Christ died to cure our "half-hearted" response to God's love. "Jesus also suffered outside the city gate to make the people holy through his own blood" (Heb. 13:12).

The Scripture declares both in type and teaching that Christ died to do an even deeper work than to justify and bring us new life. He suffered on the Cross that He might fully sanctify, make us holy. From the forgiveness of sins, we are led to the inner cleansing of the nature of sin. As we become justified and receive new life through the shedding of Jesus' blood, we also become sanctified wholly by faith in His complete sacrifice.

The Holy Spirit who convicts us of sinful acts, and prods us to confess and repent, also urges us to seek full release from the nature of sin. Our hearts hunger and thirst after righteousness (Matt. 5:6) whenever we receive the new life of the Spirit of Christ. The blood of Christ Jesus has made full atonement for our twofold sin problem, that brings forgiveness and cleansing from all sin.

John Wesley so applies our Lord's once-and-for-all sin offering to our deep need. He declares:

> Not only sin, properly so-called—that is, a voluntary transgression of a known law—but sin, improperly so-called—that is, an

involuntary transgression of a divine law, known or unknown—needs the atoning blood. I believe there is no such perfection in this life as excludes these involuntary transgressions, which I apprehend to be naturally consequent on the ignorances and mistakes inseparable from mortality. Therefore sinless perfection is a phrase I never use, lest I should seem to contradict myself. I believe a person filled with the love of God is still liable to involuntary transgressions.[8]

Through faith in Christ's atonement, a person becomes truly converted, pardoned, justified, and sanctified, made holy. Every believer enjoys this great treasure in "earthen vessels" (2 Cor. 4:7, KJV). The Holy Spirit of Christ bears witness with our spirits that we have been redeemed from the power of sin. Even so, this clear knowledge is often clouded. By some misdeed, harsh words, or harbored doubt, the sense of forgiveness may vanish. The joy of salvation becomes stifled until further pardon from the Father has been sought.

We readily admit that all people, no matter how holy, have offenses they have unconsciously committed or omitted against the perfect will of God. These offenses are not understood to be sins in the sense of willful transgression and rebellion against God. However, they are trespasses, unwitting and unintentional lapses from God's will for us.[9]

These faults should be confessed to God, as we sense them, and forgiveness sought. The joy of salvation remains only, as the gospel song says, when there is "nothing between" our "soul and the Savior." Christ shed His blood that it might "keep on cleansing" us from every sin. "But if we walk in the light, as he is in the light, we have fellowship one with another, and the blood of Jesus, his Son, purifies us from every sin" (1 John 1:7).

Genuine new birth breaks Satan's control of the human heart. Though it becomes a habitation of God through the Holy Spirit, the selfish nature of sin continues to assert itself in the Christian's life until it is renounced. A warfare persists until one's whole being becomes consecrated to God and the sin nature becomes cleansed by the blood of the Lamb and the power of His Holy Spirit.

Christ came to fully deal with our sin through His atonement. He came to provide us with a whole new stock of life. he came to implant in us His own righteous nature. Satan's power in our lives becomes cleansed, crucified, destroyed, not simply counteracted. Those who do what is sinful are of "the devil, because the devil has been sinning from the beginning. The reason the Son of God appeared was to destroy the devil's work" (1 John 3:8).

In a sense, our lives concern the matter of possession as well as ownership. I once owned a London Fog topcoat. I hung it in the lobby of a hotel restaurant, and someone took it. The coat still belonged to me, but I did not possess it. So it is that God owns us even while the devil possesses us. The obedient Christian will acknowledge Christ's ownership of him, and invites His full possession through the Holy Spirit.

As Jesus sacrificed himself to the Father's will, we must do the same. He yielded His intellect to the Father's will, and so must we. He deferred His will to that of the Father, and we must also. Christ is our example and new racial Head, using the same frail, human body, and having the same natural human drives.

Jesus Christ did all that Adam failed to do. Satan met our Lord with the same devious tactics as he used to entice Adam. Jesus came led by the Holy Spirit into the desert to be tempted by the devil. Satan tried to arouse the first suspicion when Jesus was hungry, "If you are the son of God, . . . " (Matt. 4:4). But Jesus refused to be suspicious of God the Father.

In every temptation, Christ overcame by obeying the word of His Father, and by using the Father's words in defense. The natural life of Jesus became spiritual life because He always did the Father's will. Christians must likewise obey the Lord Jesus Christ and submit their lives of nature to His holy will.

Jesus' death on the cross is the grounds whereby we receive pardon from our sins. His sacrifice also offers cleansing for our sinful natures so we can be like Him in the details of our lives. The Old Testament ceremonial sacrifice brought outward cleansing and sanctification. The writer of Hebrews declares: "How much more, then, will the blood of Christ, who through the eternal Spirit offered himself unblemished to God, cleanse our consciences from acts that lead to death, so that we may serve the living God!" (9:14).

Any selfish right to ourselves has been doubly set aside. First, we are God's because He is our creator. Nothing or no person can remove the fact that we really belong to Him. Then, by Jesus' death on the cross, we face the sacrificial price paid for our redemption. We are His because He gave His all for us.

Oswald Chambers says the "How much more . . . " in the previous scripture refers to how much more there is to know after sanctification.[10] Before entire sanctification we are simply brought to the place of knowing—we become led up to the Cross. In sanctification, we become led, as it were, through the Cross for a life of outpoured service to God. Such a life demands complete obedience day by day.

Sanctified for Obedient Service

George Muller, a devout Christian of the 19th century, became questioned about the secret of his service. He replied: "There was a day when *I died*, utterly died: died to George Muller, his opinions, preferences, tastes, and will; died to the world, its approval, or censure; died to the approval or blame even of my brethren and friends. Since then I have studied *only* to show myself approved unto God."[11]

A Christian, once identified with Jesus' sacrificial death, becomes led into the valley to be broken in service for God. We enter the path of righteousness with no right to ourselves. And we walk the way, not simply for spiritual blessings, but to be obedient and faithful servants of God like Jesus.

The approved sin offering was not some martyr's blood, not the blood of goats and bulls that had been shed, but "the blood of Christ" that forgives and cleanses. God's very life became shed for this sinful world, and His church, "which he bought with his own blood" (Acts 20:28).

All the perfections of God's essential nature were in Christ's shed blood. All of mankind's holiest and noblest attainments were in that blood.

So Jesus' death reaches the greatest and inmost sin human nature ever committed. Christ's cry from the cross, "My God, my God, why have you forsaken me?" (Matt. 27:45), is beyond our comprehension. Jesus knew and tasted to a greater extent than anyone could ever tell what it means to be separated from God by sin.

Jesus' life fully portrays the work of the Holy Spirit—"who through the eternal Spirit . . . " (Heb. 9:14). We see in Christ what the Holy Spirit will be in us if we let Him have His way in our lives. But there is a difference as well as a similarity between the Spirit in Christ and the Spirit in us. The Eternal Spirit is incarnated in Christ—never in us. The Spirit enlivens our spirits by regeneration and sanctification. He brings us into oneness with the Lord. Our consciousness is "hidden with Christ in God" (Col. 3:3).

Christ told His disciples, "If anyone would come after me, he must deny himself and take up his cross and follow me. For whoever wants to save his life will lose it, but whoever loses his life for me will find it . . . what can a man give in exchange for his soul (life)?" (Matt. 16:24-26).

Jesus Christ's life is a crucified life—one that remains dead to selfish claims. We must "deny" the right to ourselves and prefer the Divine will. At our invitation the cleansing power of the Holy Spirit works a great exchange. We "lose" our self-directed lives to gain a Spirit-controlled life. Following Christ, we, like Muller, must utterly die to self. The life force of self-will must be crucified so the Spirit of Christ can infill our hearts with total love to do God's will.

The Lord Jesus calls His followers not only to a change in life-styles, but to an exchange of life forces. That which we must give in exchange for our lives is our consent that God can have full sway in our beings. Only then can we be remade to be and do what He wills for us. Only then will new life in His Spirit flourish in obedient holiness of heart and life.

God accepts us as we rely on His Eternal Spirit who became fully incarnated in Jesus Christ. His crucifixion was the death of god incarnate. "God was in Christ reconciling the world unto himself" (2 Cor. 5:19, KJV). Only God can restore sinful people unto righteous living, and prepare them for life eternal.

The truly holy life is a God-determined life. Remember, Peter declares: "But just as he who called you is holy, so be holy in all you do; for it is written: 'Be holy, because I am holy' " (1 Pet. 1:15-16). Yet, our full obedience, our most spotless moral walking, our most earnest prayers depend on the holy ground of Christ's atonement.

Jesus made full atonement to offer us new birth and entire sanctification here and now. Zechariah's song foretold that the coming of the Christ would mean rescue from the hand of our enemies, "and to enable us to serve him without fear in holiness and righteousness before him all our days" (Luke 1:74-75).

Righteousness means living in accordance with right and justice, as enacted in our bodies, and the thoughts and attitudes expressed by our minds. John writes: "Dear children, do not let anyone lead you astray. He who does what is right is righteous, . . . The reason the Son of God appeared was to destroy the devil's work. No one who is born of God will continue to sin, . . . " (1 John 3:7-9).

The divine cure of sin is no mere bandage cover for the disease. God does impute some righteousness to us without works (Rom. 4:6). But, as Oswald Chambers insists, imputed righteousness does not mean God puts His robe of righteousness over our moral wrong, "like a snow-drift over a rubbish heap."[12] We should never surmise God pretends that we stand all right before Him when we do not.

Jesus is for us wisdom from God—"our righteousness, holiness, and redemption" (1 Cor. 1:30). Christ's very life becomes imparted to us through His atonement. We are then enabled to walk in the light of divine truth. So long as we remain in that light, God sees the perfections of His son.

Our righteousness becomes only "that which is through faith in Christ" (Phil. 3:9). The only true holiness we may claim becomes derived through faith, which the Holy Spirit uses to make us like Christ. Christian holiness, like sin, is a disposition—not a series of acts. It becomes wrought by a great exchange—the selfish nature of sin for a heart that loves to obey God. The believer receives a holy turn of mind, imparted by the Holy

Spirit. Loving obedience to God becomes the guiding trait of one's life, here and now.

Entire sanctification brings and end to the passion to sin. The process of being made righteous and holy begins the moment one becomes born of the Spirit. It becomes consummated on the unconditional surrender of a person's right to himself over to the Lordship of Jesus Christ. There is an immediate infilling of the Holy Spirit to purify the dross of selfish desires and to crucify the rebel will.

The time lapse between the new birth and the crisis of entire sanctification depends on how quickly an individual responds to the fullness of Jesus Christ's atonement. It is a pilgrimage of faith and growth in God's grace, but not growth into grace. The process of Christian growth relies on the impetus of two definite divine works of grace, justification and sanctification. The continued obedient life of a saint is enhanced by further growth and maturity in holy living.

Jesus offered himself as the supreme sacrifice for the sins of the world. He is "the Lamb of God, who takes away the sin of the world" (John 1:29). No other atoning sacrifice could suffice. Christ's death looms throughout Scripture. By faith in His death and shed blood we become partakers of His life. From this new birth we become led to seek and to receive a pure heart, which He says is required to see God (Matt. 5:8). It is no more and no less than what Christ's atonement provided.

Charles Wesley wrote in "A Perfect Heart":[13]

> O for a heart to praise my God,
> A heart from sin set free!
> A heart that always feels thy blood,
> So freely spilt for me!

NOTES

1. Frank S. Mead (ed.) *The Encyclopedia of Religious Quotations*, 27.

2. P. T. Forsyth, *The Work of Christ* (Collins, 1965), 118.

3. P. T. Forsyth, *God the Holy Father* (Independent Press, 1957), 19.

4. Milton S. Agnew, *More Than Conquerors*, 56.

5. A. M. Hunter, *P. T. Forsyth*, 63-64.

6. P. T. Forsyth, *The Cruciality of the Cross* (Grand Rapids: Wm. B. Eerdmans Publishing Co., reprint), 17.

7. Cited by Dwight H. Small, *The High Cost of Holy Living*, 72.

8. John Wesley, *Plain Account of Christian Perfection* (Chicago: Free Methodist Publishing House, n.d.), 37.

9. J. G. Morrison, *Our Lost Estate*, 55.

10. Oswald Chambers, *The Philosophy of Sin* (London: Simpkin Marshall, 1941), 17.

11. Walter B. Knight, *Master Book of New Illustrations* (Grand Rapids: Wm. B. Eerdmans Publishing Co., 1970), 111.

12. Oswald Chambers, *Conformed to His Image*, 81.

13. *Hymnal of the Methodist Episcopal Church*, 318.

CHAPTER VI

The Meaning of Jesus' Blood

In P.T. Forsyth's book, *The Cruciality of the Cross*, the final chapter is titled, "What Is Meant by the Blood of Christ?" The answer to this question becomes key to an understanding of Christ's atonement. Some proclaim the notion that Christianity is just another gory religion. The Blood flows only as a morbid element of death.

Once a preacher was speaking from the text of 1 John 1:7, "The blood of Jesus Christ his Son cleanseth us from all sin." Suddenly, he was interrupted by a skeptic, who loudly asked, "How can blood cleanse sin?"

For a moment the preacher was silent. Then he countered, "How can water quench thirst?"

"I don't know," replied the skeptic, "but I know that it does."

The preacher answered, "Neither do I know how the blood of Jesus cleanses sin, but I know it does."

Others have said it would not have mattered if not even one drop of Jesus' blood had been spilt. If He had died by poisonous hemlock or by the gallows, the sacrificial imagery would only have been changed—not the pledge of divine offering for sin. Such thinking misses the issue of divine appointment.

Since man's fall, life-giving blood has been used as the sign and the seal of a covenant pledging God's unmerited love and grace. Right after Adam's sin, God had compassion and promised redemption. He promised Adam and Eve that the power of the usurper would be broken, crushed by the seed of the woman (Gen. 3:15). God sacrificed innocent animals to make coats from their skins to cover the naked shame of that first sinful pair (3:21). That act immediately showed that human sin was a life-and-death matter.

Later, Abel's offering of the firstling of his flock (Gen. 4:4) shows the obedience of faith answering God's will of grace. That offering implies previous divine instruction (cf. 3:21), for it was "by faith" (Heb. 11:4). Since faith means taking God at His word, Cain's bloodless offering became a refusal of the Divine way.

When Noah offered burnt sacrifices after the ark landed from the Flood, the Lord savored the sacrifice and declared He would never again destroy the earth by water. He said mankind would be fruitful and replenish the earth. God put a rainbow in the sky to signal the promise set by the blood sacrifice on the altar (Gen. 8:20—9:17).

The Divine covenant became also sealed by the symbol of the blood that God would raise up a chosen people through Abraham (cf. Gen. 15:18; 17:2). Isaac, Jacob, and all of Abraham's sons were heirs to the promise. Blood became shown as a seal of the covenant in the rite of circumcision, first of Abraham, Isaac, Jacob, and of every male child of Israel.

After 430 years in Egypt, the children of Israel became delivered from bondage. Release came in junction with the sacrificial Feast of Passover. God kept His covenant with Abraham and promised to redeem His chosen people, bringing them into their own land (Exod. 6:2-9).

The Lord chose Moses to lead the people out, but Egypt's pharaoh would not release them. After sending nine plagues, God decreed the firstborn of every Egyptian family would die. Only those Israelites sheltered by blood-sprinkled doors would be saved. On the 14th day of the month, the head of every house was to slay a male yearling lamb, "without blemish," and sprinkle with hyssop the blood on the doorposts and lintel of the house. When the Lord saw the blood, He would pass over that household and smite the Egyptians with death (Exod. 12).

The pharaoh at last let the Israelites go. Their freedom and exodus proved the power of the prescribed sacrifice unto God. The Passover became an annual rite to remind the people of divine grace working in their lives. God received their obedience as a proffered life-sacrifice and reckoned the gift for public righteousness.

The Mosaic system of sin-offering required the sprinkling of a bullock's blood to make atonement for the sins of the people (Leviticus 16). But the Old Testament nowhere implies that the worth of sacrifice lies in the blood itself. Neither does it say that it resides in the suffering that goes with bloodshed. Nor does the final value rest in the life symbolized by the blood. As Forsyth says, "The value of the sacrificial rite lay wholly in the fact of its being God's will, God's appointment, what God ordained as the machinery of His grace for national purposes."[1]

On the other hand, God, from the first, sealed His salvation covenant with mankind in blood, know as the stream of life. The Lord said through Moses: "For the life of a creature is in the blood, and I have given it to you to make atonement for yourselves on the altar; it is the blood that makes atonement for one's life" (Lev. 17:11).

The meaning of all sacrifice pinpoints the offering as a seal of the sentence of the law upon the offender. Such offering anticipates the vicarious death of Jesus Christ. His sacrifice alone justifies the righteousness of God in forgiving the sins of those who offered the typical sacrifices (Exod. 29:36).

Old Testament Promise Fulfilled

Isaac Watts, in his *Praise to God for Learning to Read*, writes:

> Dear Lord, this Book of thine,
> Informs me where to go,
> For grace to pardon all my sin,
> And make me holy too.

The Old Testament sacrifices stood symbolic of the perfect One to come. They set forth in type of the "heavenly things" to be revealed (cf. Heb. 9:11, 23-25; 8:5; 10:1; Col. 2:16-17). They spoke in symbol and in prophecy of when the Christ would offer His atoning blood.

The New Testament only speaks of salvation for sinners by Jesus' life yielded upon the cross. Forgiveness is not through the blood in the veins of the sacrifice. Only the holy blood sprinkled upon the alter becomes effective. Everything turns on Jesus Christ laying down His life for us—not on His life snatched from Him.

Jesus' death stands marked with moral violence. It became imposed by human wickedness, wresting the Divine law. Full force becomes applied to both mankind's sin and Christ's redeeming blood. His death and shed blood meant more than simply a ceremony to be performed. It meant God offered a precious gift to restore the lost human race into divine love and favor.

Our Lord's life and sacrifice imbued blood with its full significance. As S. D. Gordon says, "God gave His breath to man in creation, and His blood for man on Calvary. He gave His blood because He had given His breath. Each was His very life."[2]

In a sense, the value of the "life" equals the value of "the blood" (Lev. 17:11). The blood of Jesus Christ remains precious—of inestimable value. When He shed His blood, the sinless God-man gave His life that condemned sinners might live. The writer of Hebrews declares of the Old Testament offerings: "But those sacrifices are an annual reminder of sins, because it is impossible for the blood of bulls and goats to take away sins" (10:3-4). The past public commemoration of the sins of the people became faulty. The stain of guilt remained, not completely cleansed away. The race awaited the coming Savior.

When Jesus came into the world, He said to the Heavenly Father:
> Sacrifice and offering Thou hast not desired,
> But a body Thou hast prepared for Me;
> ... 'Behold, I have come
> (In the roll of the book it is written of Me)
> To do Thy will, O God.'
> (Heb. 10:5, 7, NASB; cf. Psa. 40:6-8).

This New Testament quote from the Psalms shows Jesus knew His incarnate ministry would fulfill sacrifice. God did not desire the slaughter of beasts, but He wanted One to live before Him in perfect obedience. Only Christ's offering could meet the intent of true sacrifice.

Born as a babe, Jesus became clothed with a "body" to do the Father's will. The eternal Word became miraculously conceived in the virgin's womb and born in the likeness of mankind. Jesus shares in the flesh and blood of our humanity so by His death He might "destroy him who holds the power of death . . . " (Heb. 2:14; cf. 1 Cor. 15:50; Gal. 1:16).

The Lord and Giver of life takes no pleasure in human life's demise. Christ's death became most precious in God's sight as the crucified Savior conquered death's arrest, and freed its captives. Death became used as a transition—not extinction—because of Jesus' triumphant resurrection.

Our Lord Jesus Christ's death and resurrection seals and crowns a real moral crisis and act. His resurrection becomes the obverse of the personal crux in dying. Christ's death becomes only redemptive as a moral deed, and it is a moral conquest only as it is a crucial achievement. His shed blood means such finality. Our sin pierced the seat of life, stabbing His heart, as it were.

Jesus told His disciples the New Testament would be given in His blood (Matt. 26:28; Mark 14:23; Luke 22:20). His death at Calvary fulfilled the Old Testament promise to Adam, to Noah, and to Abram. God's salvation covenant with mankind bridged the separation of sin and death.

The New Testament word for covenant may mean a last will and testament, which becomes operative only after the testator's death. This legal sense of the term became used in the Roman world, and it remains part of our present law.[3] The Epistle to the Hebrews calls Christ the "mediator of a new covenant," and says by His death we receive "the promised eternal inheritance" (9:15). The death of the one who made the will must be proven, because a will never takes effect while the one who made it remains living (v. 16).

When soldiers at the crucifixion pierced Jesus' side to know of His death, water and blood flowed out (John 19:31-37). These elements, with the Holy Spirit, proclaim our Lord's finished work. John later wrote that the Spirit, the water, and the blood testify in agreement (1 John 5:8). Together, the Spirit and the blood confirm the new covenant is at work in our lives. "Anyone who believes in the Son of God has this testimony in his heart. . . . And this is the testimony: God has given us eternal life, and this life is in his Son" (1 John 5:10-11).

The elements of life and death conjoin in sacrifice. Amazingly, what means death, by their loss, also means life. Death-bound sinners thus find life offered by the dying Savior.

A Sacrifice of Self

A scroll of marble over a Byzantine sculpture of the figure of Christ in St. Mark's Church at Venice, Italy, contains these inscribed stirring words:

> Who He was,
> And for what purpose:
> And at what price: He redeemed thee:
> And why He did this for thee:
> And gave thee all things—
> Consider![4]

We can hardly fathom the cost of our salvation to the Divine treasure. Neither can we tell the personal anguish Jesus suffered when He offered himself to redeem us. Someone once wrote: "That which we should value in ourselves and in one another is the dignity of God's image and the great price at which we were bought." Our lives become thus inextricably tied to sacrifice.

But God doesn't seek religious tributes or presents to offset sin. His complete holiness of perfect character, love, and justice requires the offering of a total holy self, in a once-for-all gift. Only the Son sent could provide it. Jesus Christ's offering did not provide a self-sacrifice, but a sacrifice of the central self, of the whole, personal and loving self. He gave himself to life-blood sacrifice.

We may note two basic truths about the revealed concept of sacrifice. They stand in contrast and distinct from popular and pagan ideas. (1) The ground of Christ's blood atonement rests in God's grace, not in His wrath.

Positive truth declares the sacrifice marks the result of God's grace and not its cause. (2) The explanatory truth of the atonement says that the pleasing thing to God, and the effective element, anticipates not death but life.[5]

In the Old Testament, sacrificial blood became shed with the direct object, not of killing the animal, but of detaching and releasing life. The New Testament declares Jesus offered himself, bled and died that we might live. He poured out His life that we might partake of it. Christ had to die, not simply because of mankind's blindness and blunders, but because He was God's incarnate holy love. Divine holiness moving through history renders sin so sinful and mankind's wickedness so furious as to rage. The "must" of Jesus' crucifixion hinged not merely in Jewish rebels, but in the very pure nature of holiness, as it abuts human sin.

God's saving work drew blood from Christ, as it drew Him from God's very heart. Jesus shedding His blood means that what He did drew from His personality and involved His total self. Mankind's sin required the divine Son's whole being. It enjoined what remained inmost in Christ and dear to God—himself, His person, His vital soul, His blood. God's love becomes poured into our hearts only in the shedding of that most precious life-blood.

The sacrifice of Jesus Christ cannot be compared as a hero taxed to the utmost. Rather, it meant His complete obedience and surrender of His total self. Jesus' blood reached the universal moral decrees of grace that God's chosen people, Israel, were to serve and failed. The Lord Jesus met those holy requirements in a situation of racial sin.

Jesus' sacrifice became fixed as His holy character and teachings aroused the sinful world. Divine holiness must suffer in the midst of sin. This offering is not to man but for man. Sacrifice first became offered to God to hallow His name and make it honorable. The Son ever gives honor to the Father's holy love.

The Father requires assent of His perfect holiness before the confession of sin. So Christ, from His inmost being, confessed God's loving holiness, pouring out His life-blood. The Savior's true confession of holiness from the midst of sinners, whom He loved, proclaims the Divine import of His blood. Our Lord thereby provides the ground for God to accept our confession as righteous.

Divine love endures moral pain in sacrifice. Holiness also sets judgment in the earth. Sin inflicts God with pain, but He acts to judge and destroy it. Jesus' blood shed at Calvary stands for more than the string of sin on God. The Cross becomes the scourge of God on sin. Calvary not only bears God's sorrow over sin, but His wrath on it. The Cross both offers the bleeding feet that seek the sinner and marks the conflict that destroys the prince of this world, founding the holy kingdom.[6]

Religious people have thought the prime question is: How shall I feel as a child of the Heavenly Father? Rather, it is a series: How shall I stand before my judge? How shall one be just with God? What must I do to be saved? How can I be holy?

Paul says sinners become justified freely by God's mercy and grace through the redemption Christ Jesus brought. "God presented him as a sacrifice of atonement through faith in his blood. He did this to demonstrate his justice, because in his forbearance he had left the sins committed beforehand unpunished—he did it to demonstrate his justice at the present time, so as to be just and the one who justifies the man who has faith in Jesus" (Rom. 3:24-26).

Christ's submission to judgment went beyond any experience of doom and suffering as events of life. He accepted them as God's purpose, and so confessed God's perfect holiness and power as to make mankind's rage praise God. The necessity of Jesus' death became more binding by God's holiness in Him than by the evil in people it provoked.

It is not death per se that atones for our sin, but Jesus Christ's supreme act living in holy obedience. The Son's merit so meets God's loving holiness that, under the conditions of death, He provides redemption for those who believe on Him. His sacrifice creates a faith that satisfies hearts with forgiveness while meeting the justice of God.

When Jesus died at sin's hands it meant sin would slay the pure holiness of God. Sin and holiness could not live at peace in the same world. Christ rising from the grave declared that the holy God would live and reign in the world. Dying as a man, our Lord placed His whole self beside mankind under divine judgment. He joins mankind in court but on God's side of the issue, confessing God's holiness in judgment, and justifying His treatment of sin.[7]

We have no plea except by this self-justification of God. One never becomes so just with Good as when his own broken heart calls just the judgment of God. A person feels the need of justification but knows he cannot earn it. No one could ever be just with God except through God's justification of him in the blood of Jesus Christ.

Benefits of Christ's Blood

Jesus' cry from the cross, "It is finished!" became haunting. Some have viewed it as a dying utterance of despair. Christians have rightly claimed the words as a signal of victory. On the cross, giving His blood for us, Jesus made provision for the world to be saved. That sacrifice finished His mission, so mankind could be restored to God's favor.

Some natives in Central Africa speak of the death of Christ as "the victory of Golgotha." When asked why they did so, one improvised a cross with two sticks and said, "Just here at the Cross when Satan did his very worst, just then and there God did His very best. At the Cross the very worst and the very best meet."[8]

The basic gain from the blood of Christ's cross is "atonement." The Old Testament usage of the term means "to cover." The word for pitch that God told Noah to put on the ark is the word for "atonement" (Gen. 6:14). That covering held back the flood waters, making the tenants of the ark safe. Also the atoning blood of sacrifice on the altar covered the sins of the Israelites from God's view and checked His judgment.

This at-one-ment, implied in all blood sacrifices (Lev. 17:11), became affirmed on the Day of Atonement. "Yom Kippur" literally means "Day of Covering," the day set by God as the time Israel's sin became covered through His appointed sacrifice. Israel observed it annually as the climax of the Levitical year (cf. 16:2-34; 23:17-32; Num. 29:7-11). All the people stood reminded that worship of God rested upon the virtue of the blood.

But the Old Testament law and the system of animal sacrifice never really removed sin. Those obedient acts merely covered sin in lieu of the perfect sacrifice to be offered by Jesus Christ, the Lamb of God. Christ entered "the Most Holy Place once for all by his own blood, having obtained eternal redemption" (Heb. 9:12).

The blood of goats and bulls and the ashes of a heifer were annually sprinkled on those who remained ceremonially unclean to sanctify them and make them outwardly clean. "How much more, then, will the blood of Christ, who through the eternal Spirit offered himself unblemished to God, cleanse our consciences from acts that lead to death, so that we may serve the living God!" (Heb. 9:14; cf vv. 13, 25-26).

Our Lord did by His grace what the law could never do in its weakness. Our atonement becomes complete in Jesus Christ. Through Him we become truly brought into at-one-ment with God, the Father. So Paul declares, "We also rejoice in God through our Lord Jesus Christ, through whom we have now received reconciliation" (Rom. 5:11).

All sinners may find divine mercy through Jesus' atoning blood. "All have sinned and fall short of the glory of God, and are justified freely by his grace through the redemption that came by Christ Jesus. God presented him as a sacrifice of atonement, through faith in his blood" (Rom. 3:23-25).

Paul proclaims God's provision in Jesus Christ to show mercy to lost sinners. Since sin repudiates God, it spurs His judgment. Anything that scorns His nature stands condemned. God acted to remove His wrath incurred by sin, and in loving mercy extends salvation to mankind. He offers us saving grace in Jesus, the Son, who gives His life-blood. This pleases God because His own glory becomes revealed as Christ gives His life a sacrifice for His creatures.

Though God hates evil, He loves mankind, and that love consumes the defilement that would destroy him. The burning love revealed in Jesus Christ shows He loved us while we were yet sinners (Rom. 5:8). "In this is love, not that we loved God, but that He loved us and sent His Son to be the propitiation for our sins" (1 John 4:10, NASB).

The word for "propitiation" can be literally translated "mercy seat" (Heb. 9:5; cf. Exod. 25:17; Lev. 16:2, 13). It refers to the place above the Ark of the Covenant, in the Holy of Holies, where the blood of the atoning sacrifice became sprinkled. God's presence came down in "Shekinah" glory and filled the inner chamber of the tabernacle.[9]

The mercy seat covered the tablets of the covenant (Heb. 9:4; cf. Exod. 25:21). The faithful people in the Old Testament knew God's salvation had not yet come in the flesh. They looked for that time by faith, and the high priest represented them when he sprinkled the mercy seat with animal sacrifice blood.

But Jesus Christ's offering on the cross stood open to the people's view. He became crucified as a public spectacle "to be a sacrifice of atonement" (Rom. 3:25). His blood that flowed on Calvary invites us all to confess our need and turn to God in faith to receive redemption from all sin.

The blood Jesus Christ shed enables us to have a whole new relationship with God. Jesus received the judgment of our sin by taking unto himself the wrath of the Law. We become justified and forgiven as we plead the holy nature of Christ's blood. We receive divine pardon, but not because of anything we have done. It occurs for the sake of the Son who loved us and died in our stead.

When we renounce all self-righteousness and receive Jesus' love by faith, we stand before God free of sinful guilt. We no longer face condemnation, but live in Christ, the merciful and just One. "Since we have now been justified by His blood, how much more shall we be saved from God's wrath through him" (Rom. 5:9).

Atonement involves reconciliation, bringing holy God and sinful mankind together. Our at-one-ment with God comes through Christ's shed blood, and the sin that kept us from God becomes removed. Paul declares: "Therefore, if anyone is in Christ, he is a new creation; the old has gone, the new has come! All this is from God, who reconciled us to himself through Christ . . . not counting men's sins against them" (2 Cor. 5:17-19).

Faith in Christ quells our revolt against God and settles our relationship with Him. Jesus makes peace through His shed blood. We who once stood alienated from God and were enemies in our minds because of our evil behavior now become reconciled to Him. By Christ's death we are presented holy in God's sight, "without blemish and free of accusation" (Col. 1:20-22).

Our redemption occurs through Christ's precious blood. When Jesus died at Calvary, He took our place. We were all sold unto sin and under the sentence of death. But in God's matchless love, Jesus the Savior came and offered himself as our Redeemer.

The term "redemption" means to buy back or to loose. Applied to mankind, it denotes the loosing of a prisoner's bonds, setting him free. In Jesus' day, the term referred to the amount required to purchase the life of a slave. It could also apply to a ransom where a sum of money was supplied as the condition for release.[10]

The New Testament declares the blood of Christ is the purchase price of our redemption (cf. Eph. 1:7; Col. 1:14). His death became our ransom from sin (cf. Matt. 20:28; 1 Tim. 2:6). We are not redeemed with perishable things, "as silver or gold, . . . but with the precious blood of Christ, a lamb without blemish or defect" (1 Pet. 1:18-19).

Our inner nature becomes transformed through Christ's redemption. The uplifting change occurs by cleansing, "the blood of Jesus, his (God's) Son, purifies us from every sin" (1 John 1:7). This refers to the ministry of the Holy Spirit working within, purging the heart. Sin's pollution and guilt become washed away by the Savior's cleansing blood (cf. Rev. 1:5; 7:14).

Our entire being becomes cleansed from sin's defilement as the Spirit applies the Savior's blood to our lives. We still have a frail and corrupt human nature, and we live in a wicked world that multiplies temptation to sin. But our spirits and lives remain clean as we abide in Christ. When we walk in His light, obey His will, His blood keeps us pure moment by moment.

In cleansing our hearts, the holy Spirit imparts the Divine nature, filling us with divine love. Jesus suffered "outside the city gate to make his people holy through his own blood" (Heb. 13:12). Our sanctification implies obedience and consecration to God's will, being set apart for His use, sharing in his purity and love.

Jesus Christ committed himself to the mission of the Cross that we might be redeemed and sanctified through the truth (John 17:9). His blood marks His total obedience to the will of the Father. By the same token, it calls us to a life of full surrender and obedience (1 Pet. 1:2).

The supreme ministry of the Holy Spirit moves to reveal Jesus Christ to us. To know Christ aright means we have everlasting life. The Savior's shed blood remains the central focus of the Spirit's work, and He applies the benefits of that sacrifice to every believer. Just as the Holy Spirit enabled Christ to offer himself for us, He constrains us to submit our lives to Him. Through faith in Christ we become transformed into His likeness with ever-increasing glory. The Spirit abides and keeps our lives pure by His power (2 Cor. 3:18).

At the heart of the Holy Spirit's power is the witness of divine forgiveness. The blood of Christ signifies a holy virtue that quickens every aspect of our lives. Those who believe in Him find gracious access into a redeemed life. It becomes a matter of trusting in divine provision for salvation instead of ourselves.

Louisa M. R. Stead penned this poignant truth in her hymn: " 'Tis So Sweet to Trust in Jesus."

> 'Tis so sweet to trust in Jesus,
> Just to take Him at His word;
> Just to rest upon His promise;
> Just to know, "Thus saith the Lord."
>
> Oh, how sweet to trust in Jesus,
> Just to trust His cleansing blood;
> Just in simple faith to plunge me
> 'Neath the healing, cleansing flood!
>
> Yes, 'tis sweet to trust in Jesus,
> Just from sin and self to cease;
> Just from Jesus simply taking
> Life and rest, and joy and peace.

How quickly our lives become so complex, demanding that we must trust someone—perhaps ourselves! All too soon, both we and our friends fail to qualify. The paths of life—and death—run far beyond us. Only Jesus

Christ can bear our every burden. He says, "Hand it over to me: I will take care of it."

Because Jesus died and shed His blood for us, we can bow before Him and say, "Here is my life Lord, both the good and the bad; every problem and every ambition I give to you." Hold out your hands as though they contained everything, and give it over to Christ. Let Him take it, and trust Him with the whole bundle. "Calvary covers it all."

NOTES

1. P. T. Forsyth, *The Cruciality of the Cross*, 86.
2. S. D. Gordon, *Quiet Talks with World Winners* (New York: Fleming H. Revell Co., 1908), 24.
3. Robert E. Coleman, *Written in Blood* (Old Tappan, N.J.: Fleming H. Revell Co., 1972), 100.
4. G. B. F. Hallock, *2500 Best Modern Illustrations* (New York: Harper & Brothers Publishers, 1935), 49.
5. P. T. Forsyth, *The Cruciality of the Cross*, 89.
6. Cf. Ibid., 99-100.
7. Cf. Ibid., 102.
8. Cf. Walter B. Knight, *Master Book of New Illustrations*, 151.
9. Robert E. Coleman, *Written in Blood*, 109.

CHAPTER VII

The Holy Virtue of Forgiveness

In his hymn, "Joyful, Joyful, We Adore Thee" (v. 3), Henry Van Dyke praises God's forgiveness:

> Thou art giving and forgiving,
> Ever blessing, ever blest,
> Well-spring of the joy of living
> Ocean depth of happy rest!
> Thou our Father, Christ our brother—
> All who live in love are Thine.
> Teach us how to love each other;
> Lift us to the joy divine.

One cannot calculate the power of forgiveness in forging the integration of human personalities. God alone knows how many demons are being cast out, how many mental problems, neuroses, and organic diseases become squelched by the assurance of divine pardon and renewal. Leslie D. Weatherhead rightly claims the forgiveness of God is the most powerful therapeutic idea in the world.

Forgiveness stands indeed a divine virtue—one of the first blessings we receive from God. His kiss of pardon marks the change from the old to the new life in Christ. The word and pledge of God's love prepares us to receive all the spiritual gifts offered in Christ Jesus. They are to sustain our relationship with Him—in life or death.

Charles Haddon Spurgeon once stood preaching about Stephen, the first Christian martyr. An unbeliever questioned Spurgeon, asking, "What did God do to help Stephen when he was being stoned to death?"

Spurgeon had a ready answer. He replied, "God enabled Stephen to pray, 'Lord, lay not this sin to their charge.' "[1]

Such forgiveness goes beyond normal human response. Andrew Murray names forgiving love as one of the greatest marvels revealed in the Divine nature. God wants His redeemed people to share in the glory to which He has called them. As they have received forgiveness through Christ, they are to forgive others who wrong them.[2]

When God extends forgiving love to us, it is not just to redeem us from punishment. He seeks to implant a loving spirit in us, to indwell and sustain its righteous character and honest beauty in our personal relationships. Forgiving love seeks to do its work in and through us, leading and enabling us to pardon those who sin against us.

Both early and modern Christians have faced two pointed questions: (1) Is forgiveness necessary? and (2) Is forgiveness possible? Amid the agelong human struggle with temptation and sin, every new generation receives the gospel. Despite the barrier of doubts, whenever and wherever the Church truly proclaims the forgiveness of sins, healing occurs.[3]

Yet mankind often becomes victim of the illusion that he doesn't need forgiveness. Some who hear the Christian gospel and its offer of divine pardon would ridicule: "Forgiveness? For me? What do I need it for? What have I done that I should be forgiven? Others have blundered and made a mess of things— this is why the world is in such a sordid plight—but I am not to blame!"

Some do not attempt forgiveness because they don't believe in the reality of sin. How is such a false shelter to be leveled? How do we rebut those who join Benedict de Spinoza in his *Ethics*, who announced, "Evil is nothing positive"?[4] They doubt any Power is behind the universe who cares how they run their lives. It has more important things to do. God will simply pat the sinner on the head and say, "There, there! You didn't mean it. It doesn't matter much!"

Some thus think of forgiveness as not necessary. They merely place it in reserve for those who have a psychological need.

This romantic myth about human nature gave support to the Victorian gospel of inevitable progress. Such naive utopianism remains just an old denial of sin's reality, posed in a new guise.

No amount of contradictory evidence seems to disrupt modern mankind's high opinion of himself. The idealism of secular humanism overlooks personal responsibility and pins human ills on lack of development. Mankind in general forgets the savage demon in his heart, and the anarchic passions of his soul.

But those who minimize sin and deny the need of forgiveness sometimes have twinges of unrest and self-reproach. Like Emil Brunner declares, "The bad conscience is like a dog which is shut up in the cellar on account of its tiresome habit of barking, but is continually on the watch to break into the house which is barred against him, and is able to do so the moment the master's vigilance is relaxed."[5]

No person who has really known the chaos of the world, and of his own heart, can long pretend forgiveness remains unnecessary.

Christ Makes Forgiveness Necessary

Jesus of Nazareth, as an actual historical personality, has indelibly impressed the conscience and the imagination of all mankind. The standards of conduct associated with His name have become respected and honored far beyond the confines of His Church. A particular occasion tells about a Hindu and a Moslem who were arguing a case before an Indian judge. One suddenly declared a certain act was "un-Christlike." The term at once placed a hush upon the court. From that point it seemed granted that the final word had been spoken, without any need for further argument. The moral stature of Jesus became acknowledged without question or reproach.[6]

The authority of Jesus has not declined with the passing centuries. People seldom wash their hands of His message and presence to get rid of

Him. Pontius Pilate tried—and failed. There is that strange "King of the Jews" upon His cross who draws one back to righteousness again and again.

The stunning compassion of Jesus Christ pierces the human dilemma of those who would rationalize away sin. Though liberal theology has dismissed the doctrine of original sin, the historical plight still etches that truth into the restless conscience of the race. Christ's coming to save us from our sins demands we seek divine pardon for them.

Notice how often and how expressly the Lord Jesus spoke of forgiveness. He taught His disciples to pray: "Forgive us our debts, as we also have forgiven our debtors" (Matt. 6:12). He goes on to say, "But if you do not forgive men their sins, your Father will not forgive your sins" (v. 15).

Peter asked Jesus: "Lord, how many times shall I forgive my brother when he sins against me? Up to seven times?"

Jesus answered, "I tell you, not seven times, but seventy times seven" (Matt. 18:21-22).

Christ also told His disciples, "And when you stand praying, if you hold anything against anyone, forgive him, so that your Father in heaven may forgive you your sins" (Mark 11:25). God's forgiveness of us thus hinges on our forgiveness of others.

After the Lord Jesus Christ ascended on high to grant repentance and forgiveness of sins, Scripture says of Him just what He had said of the Father. We must forgive like Him. Paul writes: "Bear with each other and forgive whatever grievances you may have against one another. Forgive as the Lord forgave you" (Col. 3:13).

Forgiveness becomes love in action. It is the only soil from which a holy life can grow. We are told if we don't forgive it becomes a sure sign that we ourselves have not been forgiven. And one who only seeks pardon selfishly, to escape punishment, has not truly allowed forgiving love to rule his heart and life. God's forgiveness in Christ has never really reached him.

But when we accept divine forgiveness we also find joy in forgiving others. Faith in God's personal forgiveness becomes confirmed. We receive forgiveness from Christ and, like Him, bestow it to others. We become forgiven to be forgiving, passing on the divine love we have received.

Judy Lawson, a committed Christian, became faced with such a seemingly impossible mission. Her oldest son, Dean, was murdered at a drug deal in early 1976. Judy felt compelled to pray for the two men charged in her son's killing. She admitted, "In the flesh I might have torn them limb from limb. But I didn't want hate, anger, or revenge in my life."

In time, Judy sensed she was to pray specifically for Richard Wine. "God . . . . asked me to love Richard for Him, and I asked to see Richard through God's eyes."

May 1976, Richard received a "25-years-plus-life" sentence and became shipped to Lake Butler Reception Center in north Florida. Just days later Judy was at Lake Butler for a parole hearing of a relative. Among the 60 inmates that entered the room, she saw Richard among them. Judy quickly walked over to him, gently touching him on the arm. "Richard, I'm Dean's mother," she said. He looked at her in amazement asking her how she could touch him.

"Richard, God loves you and wants to forgive you," she told him. A guard hurried Judy away, as Richard asked, "How could you ever forgive me?"

Judy wrote to Richard and prayed for him for more than four years—years he spent looking into Eastern religions, running drugs, and ending up at Florida State Prison. Prisoners call that institution "the end of the line."

In the fall of 1980, during a stint in solitary confinement, Richard's choice of reading material was the Bible or nothing at all. He read the entire book in 11 days. "By the time I got to Isaiah 42 the Lord was speaking to me," he said. "I knew there was hope, another way to live."

Thanksgiving Day 1980, after reading through the Gospels, Richard knelt beside his bed and repented of his sins, asking Jesus Christ to take over his life.[7]

God's forgiveness must be confirmed through the forgiving acts of His people. Though friends and family find it difficult to understand, as was the case with Judy Lawson, God calls us to be channels of Divine love to the most unloving person. We have the joy of God's pardon only as we forgive those who have wronged us.

Jesus Christ's own holy character makes forgiveness necessary. Some dare to say, "I may not be a saint, but I'm at least as good as so and so." That excuse wilts before the blameless daily beauty of Christ's life, and causes one to see his ugly self.

Augustine, when a young scholar in the University of Carthage, became self-indulgent and complacent. In his *Confessions*, he declares: "There sang around me in my ears a caldron of unholy loves."

One day Jesus crossed his fickle path, and he became humbled to the dust. Augustine cried, "You took me from behind my own back, where I had put myself all the time that I preferred not to see myself. And you set me there before my face that I might see how vile I was . . . . I saw myself and was horrified."[8]

The perfect holiness of Christ shatters pride and revokes a person's self-righteous rule. Dare we bring our lives into the white light of the character of Jesus—compared to His matchless nobility, to His measureless spirituality—and think we have nothing to be forgiven? The brightness of Christ's pure holiness becomes like a lightning flash across the midnight of our self-deceptions.

The cross of Christ forever makes forgiveness necessary. The apostles preached and wrote, showing people the cross of Christ, and their part in His crucifixion. The One who cried, "Forgive them!" from the cross remains the One who prompts His followers to forgive, as they have been forgiven.

E. Stanley Jones once told of the conversion of a government official in India. the man's work often took him away from home. He became tempted, and he fell into shame. As time passed, his guilt tormented him. One day he called his wife into the room and began disclosing the whole wretched story. As the meaning dawned on her, she turned deathly pale, staggered against the wall, and crumpled with tears streaming down her face.

"In that moment," the man said afterwards, "I saw the meaning of the Cross. I saw love crucified by sin." After a time, she said she still loved him and would not leave him but help him back to a new life. He soon became converted—saved by cross-bearing forgiveness.[9]

Again, we too, must forgive as the Lord has forgiven us. If we withhold forgiveness, our Heavenly Father will not forgive us. God seeks to conquer evil through forgiving love. What Christ has done in forgiving evildoers from the Cross must be the standard of our conduct. Only by following His example do we show we have truly received forgiveness of sins.

The vicious acts that nailed Christ to the cross now wreck the world as common sins of daily living. Self-centeredness, pride, apathy, contempt, looseness, and bitterness, supplied the spikes and prompted the spear-thrust at Calvary. Can anyone deny, with Jesus hanging there, that sin remains the ruthless enemy, the most perilous craving in the world, and that a sinner needs to be forgiven and cleansed?

Our plight would be utterly hopeless if Jesus Christ only exposed sin and made forgiveness necessary. His holy sacrifice also becomes the source of our salvation unto eternal life.

Christ Makes Forgiveness Possible

Victor Whitechurch's book, *The Locum Tenans*, tells of a tragic refusal of forgiveness. The husband became greatly wronged by his wife, whom he passionately loved. He accidently reenters her life after an absence of more than 20 years, and finds her dying.[10]

She craves forgiveness. "Henry," she said, "I am dying." The husband raised his head almost imperceptibly. "You . . . you . . . you loved me once," she said chokingly. He stood unmoved and aloof from her who sought what only he could give her—forgiveness. "It is because I am dying. I ask, I suppose, too hard a thing. You cannot, oh, you cannot forgive!"

He straightened himself, but remained silent. He did not look down at her again, or so much as turn his head. He kept it averted from her as he quickly crossed the sickroom, opened the door and vanished. Desperately, she watched him to the last, her eyes a-starting from her head, her hands clutching each other convulsively. But he had gone—never to return.

Turning from the heartless chaos of the world and the clutches of sin, we ask: "Is forgiveness really possible?" Our lives seem held by the rigid law of cause and effect. A saying declares, "As one makes his bed, so must he lie in it." As he has acted, so he must bear the consequences. The past has gone and remains out of human control.

Where is forgiveness to be found? How can it ever enter the hopeless cycle? Pardon seems impossible.

Every evil deed a person casts into the stream of life becomes like a stone falling into a river: the ripples spread out unchecked, in widening circles, reaching the farthest shore. Evil thus propagates itself relentlessly. Before sinners become aware, it becomes rampant and beyond control.

How can forgiveness break the chain of wrongdoing with redemption? There seems to be no opportunity.

As James S. Stewart points out, the great masters of literature—from Aeschylus and Sophocles down to Shakespeare and Dostoevsky—have declared: "There is no road back to where you started from. That day, years ago, you made your choice: and today it is burning your hands, and you would like to throw it away, but you can't."[11]

The tragic thing about sin is not that it fails of its goal, but it succeeds all too well. One's life remains comprised of choices—he has to choose, and he chooses as he does. He gets what he has chosen and ends up chained to it. The Psalmist declared God gave the children of Israel "their request; but sent leanness into their soul" (Psa. 106:15, KJV).

From diverse angles, the idea has become deeply rooted that forgiveness is not possible. So the *Rubaiyat of Omar Khayyam* asserts:

> The Moving Finger writes; and having writ,
>   Moves on: nor all thy Piety nor Wit
> Shall lure it back to cancel half a Line.
>   Nor all thy Tears wash out a Word of it.[12]

One thing stands sure, divine forgiveness does not mean "letting off," excused of responsibility. We fail to understand the gospel of Christ if we think this is the chief concern. Pardon rarely means escaping all the consequences of sin. Indeed, the prodigal son became forgiven, but that didn't erase the need for time-consuming readjustment and rehabilitation. Scripture at least suggests the tense relationship with the elder brother.

The crucial point is that sin's penalty affects a forgiven person differently than one who has not accepted divine forgiveness. Whatever a forgiven person must suffer may be viewed as for a creative purpose, in positive cooperation with God. Judgment itself will seem transformed. It will be seen as mercy and not wrath.

Though the prodigal son had to face the results of squandered inheritance, he returned home. Even if bitter things had to be endured, what really mattered was that the broken relationship with his father had been restored. It did not mean the remission of a penalty, but a restored relation by undeserved forgiveness. Beyond the biblical parable, is it really possible for one's lost relationship with God to be renewed? We have the testimony of God's true forgiveness by the apostles. Paul declared, "It is written: 'I believed; therefore I have spoken.' With that same spirit of faith we also believe and therefore speak, because we know that the one who raised the Lord Jesus from the dead will also raise us with Jesus and present us with you in his presence" (2 Cor. 4:13-14).

One day Richard Baxter, Puritan scholar and writer, saw a murderer being marched through the streets to execution. He pondered the sad sight for a moment, and then said to a friend, "There goes Richard Baxter, but for the grace of God!"[13] Viewing the sorry state of any guilty criminal, each of us could say, "There I go, but for the grace of God!"

Thomas Chalmers once asked: "What could I do if God did not justify the ungodly?"[14] The question haunts every penitent sinner.

The testimony of the forgiven in effect banks on the seeking love of God. It expresses the hope and faith that He will in fact forgive for Jesus' sake. The priceless gift of the worthy Savior makes forgiveness possible to whomever accepts it by faith. The apostles thus dared to counter the world's denial of the possibility of forgiveness. Their proclamation stemmed from the words: " . . . the God and Father of our Lord Jesus Christ" (Rom. 15:6); " . . . the gospel about Jesus Christ, the Son of God" (Mark 1:1).

The Graeco-Roman world of the first century became haunted by the spirits of the dead and the whimsical gods of nature. Many still feel bound to fate, to their horoscope, and even to the elemental spirits and the invisible powers that influence our world. More than ever, the human predicament cries for divine deliverance. Though people become inclined to believe natural law rules the universe, God remains the personal Spirit with creative love.

We have every reason to believe God wants to forgive, to create a new situation for the sinful. Those who say He can't forgive do not prevent the miracle of His saving grace. A wonderful discovery awaits all who hunger and thirst after God's righteousness.

In his book, *Grace Abounding*, John Bunyan declared: "By His grace there came occasionally calling after me, these words, 'I have blotted out, as a thick cloud, thy transgressions, and, as a cloud, thy sins: return unto me; for I have redeemed thee' (Isa. 44:22, KJV). And this would make me stop a little, and, as it were, look over my shoulder behind me to see if I could discern that the God of grace still followed me with a pardon in His hand."[15]

God offers us His forgiveness when we can hardly believe it possible, thinking that we have sinned away our day of grace. Faust, in an old story, gambled with his soul. An artist painted a picture—a game of chess—Faust at one side, Satan at the other. The artist depicts the game as almost over. Faust has only a few pieces left—the king, a knight, and a couple of pawns. His drawn face expresses awful despair. At the other side of the board the devil leers, anticipating his triumph. Many chess players had looked at the picture and agreed that the position looked hopeless—it meant checkmate.

One day a great chess master came to the gallery and studied the painting. He became struck by the anguish of defeat lining the face of Faust. Then the master gazed at the position of the chess pieces on the board. He became absorbed, seeking a possible move. Other visitors came and went as he pondered. Suddenly, people in the gallery became startled by a ringing shout: "It's a lie! The game is not lost! The king and the knight have another move!"[16]

The same is true with our plight—our struggle with sin and Satan. With Christ, our King, we have another move to victory. His power and authority by His life, death, and resurrection provide for our forgiveness and life. There is a way of escape from the tempter's trap. The divine virtue of His holiness transforms us and offers hope where there was no hope in our own human strength.

Not only is our forgiveness of sin possible before God, but we become enabled to forgive those who sin against us. Jesus Christ came to make pardon possible in both respects. Neither habits of sin nor Satan himself can prevent our new life by faith in Christ.

The Life of Pardon

Below Victoria Falls, across the Zambezi River flowing through South Africa, is a bridge that spans a chasm known as the widest and most turbulent waters seen on any river in the world. That bridge construction required building an arm out from either shore. The two outstretched arms became joined in the center, over the roaring river. Neither arm could have reached the other bank by itself; the two had to meet each other. So also must our penitence and divine pardon meet to bridge the awful gulf that separates a sinner from God. Pardon without penitence is not possible, and penitence without pardon becomes useless.[17]

The Christian Church, from the first, has urged sinners to repent of their sins to receive God's pardon. But in turn, the Church has been asked: "Is forgiveness the right way to live?" Modern evangelism faces the same issue. God's call to righteous living remains clear. Christians become led to not only forgive just as Christ did, but to make it the rule of their daily conduct.

God does not freely forgive our sins to encourage our sinning. Rather, He forgives to deliver from sin's bondage. Christ bore our sin and guilt on Calvary. This makes us responsible to accept His transforming grace by faith. Paul says, "Shall we go on sinning so that grace may increase? By no means! We died to sin; how can we live in it any longer?" (Rom. 6:1-2).

Some have questioned the ethics of any act of forgiveness, suggesting God's pardon dismisses sin. Nothing could be further from the truth. God never meets our guilty distress like a person who says to his wayward neighbor, "Never mind, it is no big deal." Such a tack would degrade all moral values in the world.

Forgiveness is what reveals God's absolute righteousness. At Christ's cross of sacrifice divine pardon is bestowed to endorse God's wrath against sin. The hatefulness of sin becomes exposed in the very act of cleansing it away. The Christian doctrine of atonement shows us that sin has dreadful results and is a terrible reproach to God.

James Denney rightly says, "To take the condemnation out of the Cross is to take the nerve out of the Gospel."[18] This explains why Jesus strongly rebuked Peter's blunder at Caesarea Philippi to deflect Him from His mission of suffering. To offer the world redemption by an easier road than Calvary would obscure the just judgment of pure holiness on evil, compromise the very nature of God, and leave mankind to a merciless universe of caprice and chaos.

God didn't annul sin when Jesus Christ, God incarnate, opposed it with His life and condemned it with His death. The fearsome points of divine judgment on sin were not repealed as though mercy canceled out justice. Rather, the Son of God himself brought justice and mercy together, dying for our sins. This cost of forgiveness, one we could never meet, refutes forever any charge that forgiveness is cheap grace. It remains sealed by the holy blood of the Lord Jesus.

Though free divine pardon seems to condone sin and withdraw restraint from the sinner, it has an opposite effect. Forgiveness becomes one of the greatest forces for righteousness in the world. It was for Peter after his denial of Christ. Jesus' resurrection meant new life that included complete pardon to restore and redirect ruined lives.

During the third post resurrection appearance to the disciples, Jesus used a breakfast to reinstate Peter from the depths of his triple disavowal. The probing of the Master laid bare the hurt, but offered healing. "Jesus said to Simon Peter, 'Simon son of John, do you truly love me more than these?' "

"Yes, Lord," he said, "you know that I love you."

Jesus said, "Feed my lambs. . . . Take care of my sheep. . . . Feed my sheep. . . . Follow me!" (John 21:15-19).

Christ thus commissioned Peter anew, and put His work back into the hands of the one He had called "Cephas, the Rock" (John 1:42). This divine acceptance and trust transformed broken and unstable Peter. The devious private demon that had pushed him to the brink of ruin became thwarted.

By the purging and infilling with the Holy Spirit at Pentecost, Peter became the flaming and steadfast apostle of the Book of Acts. He defied the religious challenge of Annas and Caiaphas. Scripture reveals the ongoing regenerative force of divine pardon and cleansing. This became a moral power that girded Peter against the temptations of the world.

From the depths of his heart, Peter lived out the words: "O Jesus, my Lord and Master, who has trusted and forgiven me—I vow, God helping me, I will never, never break my loyalty to You again!"

Philosopher Soren Kierkegaard describes his own salvation experience in his *Journals*:

> I am a poor wretch whom God took charge of, and for whom He had done so indescribably much more that I only long for the peace of eternity in order to do nothing but thank Him. As a man, personally I am, in a more than general sense, a sinner who has been far along the road to perdition—a sinner who nevertheless believes that all his sins are forgiven him for Christ's sake, even though he must bear the result of punishment; a sinner who longs for eternity in order to thank Him and His love.[19]

That redeeming love becomes a creative power that sanctifies, makes holy, the first act of divine justification. The pardoned person unites himself in gratitude to the Christ who endured the cross and despised the shame to become the Savior of the world.

God used Calvary to evoke our repentance, to remold our wills, and to redeem the whole sinful situation. He broke into the tragic sequence of sin's blinding and hardening effects, which lead to deeper wickedness. His loving sacrifice shatters the vicious cycle in which all mankind has been bound and helpless.

Christ's cross did not stand as the grotesque emblem of His defeat by sin and Satan. Divine purpose used it to arrest the agelong malignant spread of iniquity throughout the human race. The Cross transformed the seeming triumph of evil into the means of redeeming grace. The power of this suffering came through the blood Jesus shed in forgiveness. Divine pardon turns evil to good, and the wrath of mankind to the praise of God.

Thankfully, the gospel of God's forgiveness doesn't depend on being understood. It remains really beyond comprehension. But our pardon relies on our faith that takes it like a little child—of such is the Kingdom of heaven. Faith must believe all that God says and does is right. "Without faith it is impossible to please God, . . . " (Heb. 11:6).

Though faith doesn't know where it will be led, it knows and loves the One who now leads. Faith thus embraces the whole being of the person who seeks to be rightly related to God. By the power of the Spirit of Jesus, faith lays claim to the whole man and all that God's grace can make him.[20]

When Jesus saw the simple faith of the men who brought a paralytic to Him for healing, He said to the paralytic, "Courage, your sins are forgiven" (Matt. 9:2, MOFFATT).

By faith we take new heart in life, both in the act of receiving or giving forgiveness. The Holy Spirit of Christ clothes us with redeeming grace to live a righteous life as God purposed. His loving presence arms us to impact this sinful world with a holy crusade.

God imputes faith for righteousness to every believer. We become justified by faith in the righteousness of Christ, not by works. God justifies the believer for the sake of Christ's righteousness, and not for any of our own. Jesus Christ procured righteousness for us by His obedience. Every believer becomes forgiven and accepted by God merely for the sake of what Christ has done and suffered. As John Wesley declares, we must put off the filthy rags of our own righteousness before we can put on the spotless righteousness of the Lord Jesus Christ.[21]

Wesley anticipates the holy virtue of forgiveness in the following verse:

> While thus we bestow
> Our moments below,
> Ourselves we forsake,
>
> And refuge in Jesus' righteousness take.
>
> His passion alone,
> The foundation we own;
> And pardon we claim,
>
> And eternal redemption in Jesus' name.[22]

NOTES

1. A. Gordon Nasby (ed.), *1041 Sermon Illustrations, Ideas, and Expositions*, 120.
2. Andrew Murray, *Like Christ* (New York: Fleming H. Revell Co., n.d.), 140-141.
3. Cf. James S. Stewart, *A Faith to Proclaim*, 51-72.
4. Cited in Ibid., 52.
5. Cited in Ibid., 53.
6. Cf. A. Gordon Nasby (ed.), *1041 Sermon Illustrations, Ideas, and Expositions*, 26.
7. *Jubilee*, The Monthly Newletter of Prison Fellowship, February 1985, 1, 4.
8. Augustine, *Confessions*, III, 1.
9. Cited in James S. Stewart, *A Faith to Proclaim*, 58.
10. Cf. A. Gordon Nasby (ed.), *1041 Sermon Illustrations, Ideas, and Expositions*, 119.
11. James S. Stewart, *A Faith to Proclaim*, 60.
12. Cited in Ibid., 61.
13. Cited in Ibid., 63.
14. Cited in Ibid.
15. John Bunyan, *Grace Abounding* (Chicago: Moody Press, 1959), 60-61.
16. Cited in James S. Stewart, *A Faith to Proclaim*, 65-66.
17. G.B.F. Hallock, *2500 Best Modern Illustrations*, 265.
18. *Expositor's Bible*, Second Epistle to the Corinthians, 222.
19. Soren Kierkegaard, *Journals*, 257.
20. Oswald Chambers, *Conformed to His Image*, 51.
21. John Wesley, *Works* (Grand Rapids: Zondervan Publishing House, n.d.), V, 241.
22. Ibid., 242.

CHAPTER

VIII

Forgiveness, Consecration, and Cleansing

Some have said the desert is a desert because no rain falls on it. But that tells only half of the truth. No rain falls on the desert because it is a dry desert. The warmed air rushing up from the hot arid surface scatters the vapors that would gather and descend in raindrops. There must be some moisture on earth, else rain cannot form and fall from the clouds. So our hearts need a forgiving disposition. Without it we cannot rejoice in the fullness of God's forgiving grace.

New Testament writers use the term "grace" to describe the spontaneous, beautiful, unearned love of God at work in Jesus Christ through the Holy Spirit. The Greek word for grace is *charis*, which means "beauty, charm, attractiveness." The gospel sense came to include "favor, kindness, and gratitude" as felt by the receiver. Grace means both the free, forgiving love of God in Christ to sinners and that love acting in the lives of Christians.

Considering "The Power of Grace," we may use the letters of the word "grace" as an acrostic.[1]

"G" stands for *God*, the Source of grace. Peter exhorts his readers that "the God of all grace, who called you to His eternal glory in Christ, will Himself perfect, confirm, strengthen and establish you" (1 Pet. 5:10, NASB).

"R" suggests *redemption*, the purpose of grace: "In him we have redemption through his blood, the forgiveness of sins, in accordance with the riches of God's grace that he lavished on us with all wisdom and understanding" (Eph. 1:7-8).

"A" is for *abundance*, the measure of grace: "And God is able to make all grace abound to you, so that in all things at all times, having all that you need, you will abound in every good work" (2 Cor. 9:8).

"C" points to *Christ*, the Mediator of grace: "For you know the grace of our Lord Jesus Christ, that though he was rich, yet for your sakes he became poor, so that you through his poverty might become rich" (2 Cor. 8:9).

"E" speaks of *eternity*, the duration of grace: "But where sin increased, grace increased all the more, so that, just as sin reigned in death, so also grace might reign through righteousness to bring eternal life through Jesus Christ our Lord" (Rom. 5:20-21).

Clearly, our salvation comes completely of divine grace, and none of our own works. Grace is commonly defined as "the unmerited favor or mercy of God." But we must not stop with His gift of justification, as wonderful as it is, and miss the full thrust of the gospel. We become justified by God's grace so we may be purified in "grace-full living."

Two basic crisis experiences become essential to spiritual life. An unconverted person must be born anew before he can have life in God. One justified must be baptized with the Holy Spirit if he is to know the fullness of life.[2] Paul says: "Since we live by the Spirit, let us keep in step with the Spirit" (Gal. 5:25).

God's grace not only provides pardon from sin; it also supplies power for righteous living. His grace includes more than saving grace for a forgiven past; it is a sanctifying grace for a transformed present and future for the lives of believers. Paul declared to Titus:

> For the grace of God that brings salvation has appeared to all men. It teaches us to say "No" to ungodliness and worldly passions, and to live self-controlled, upright and godly lives in this present age,

while we wait for the blessed hope—the glorious appearing of our great God and Savior, Jesus Christ, who gave himself for us to redeem us from all wickedness and to purify for himself a people that are his very own, eager to do what is good (Titus 2:11-14).

This passage unfolds the full scope of divine grace. God's grace sought us though we had strayed far from Him. His grace has "appeared to all men," coming to a person's heart before one has turned to accept the Savior. Some people call such mercy "prevenient grace."

The grace of God in Christ rescues us from the clutches of sinful habits, and pardons from all iniquity. That grace further works to sanctify, cleanse, and purify us to renounce "ungodliness and worldly passions." It is a second definite crisis and ongoing divine action that enables weak believers to "live self-controlled, upright and godly lives in this present age" (2:12).

This same grace sustains us to be "eager to do what is good" while we look "for the blessed hope—the glorious appearing of our great God and Savior, Jesus Christ" (2:13).

Jesus had said, "Heaven and earth will pass away, but my words will never pass away" (Luke 21:33). Though all His words are meaningful and eternal, none become more precious than those He spoke to Paul: "My grace is sufficient for you, for my power is made perfect in weakness" (2 Cor. 12:9).

God's forgiving love in Christ remains freely offered to sinners, and it seasons and sustains the lives of Christians. We become forgiven to be forgiving. Christ gave His all that we might submit our all to Him in consecration. We become justified by His grace so we may be cleansed—redeemed to live in obedience to Him throughout our lives. Nothing in this lost and ruined world bears the meek but powerful impress of the Lord Jesus so surely as forgiveness.

Forgiven to Become Saints

A Christian convert in Botswana, enthused in his newly found faith, exclaimed: "The cross of Christ condemns me to become a saint!"

That witness disclosed an important truth. The true purpose of the Savior's death and the real object of a Christian's life become revealed. As forgiveness became one of the first things Jesus did for us, our forgiveness of others becomes one of the first acts we will do for Him.

The object to which the Cross points is not simply the forgiveness of sins, a title to heaven, and deliverance from the wrath to come, but to a Christlike walk. Paul writes: "And you also are among those who are called to belong to Jesus Christ. . . . who are loved by God and called to be saints: . . . " (Rom. 1:6-7).

Also, to the church in Corinth, the Apostle writes: " . . . to those sanctified in Christ Jesus and called to be holy [saints, KJV], together with all those everywhere who call on the name of our Lord Jesus Christ—their Lord and ours: . . . " (1 Cor. 1:2).

God has indeed called us to be saints—to be holy—to walk before Him in loving obedience, as Jesus did. Pardon, happiness, and heaven all remain subordinate to sainthood. Holiness remains the personal element in which salvation and heaven are to be found. In a very real sense, the Cross does "condemn" you and me to be saints. God calls every Christian to be holy.

Paul's own life exemplifies that truth. The Apostle proclaims the greatest power in stirring human gratitude and devotion remains the forgiveness achieved by the sacrifice of the Father and the Son. To know oneself forgiven at so awesome a cost first sends a person to his knees in utter remorse, and then sets him upon his feet, ready for God's holy command.

How the Cross brings mankind pardon stands unexplained. But the fact itself becomes firmly proclaimed by the apostles. Peter declared: "The God of our fathers raised Jesus from the dead—whom you had killed by hanging him on a tree. God exalted him to his own right hand as Prince and Savior that he might give repentance and forgiveness of sins to Israel" (Acts 10:43).

Jesus himself gives every warrant to connect His death on the cross with the forgiveness of sins. He said, "For even the Son of Man did not come to be served, but to serve, and to give his life a ransom for many" (Mark 10:45). During His last supper, the Lord offered the wine-cup to His disciples, and said, "This is my blood of the covenant, which is poured out for many" (Mark 14:24). The earliest Christian proclamation, "Christ died for our sins," carried the Master's own authority.

How Jesus' death on the cross mediates our forgiveness remains hard to define. But that it does provide our pardon relies on Christ's own word and meets the inmost instinct of a longing heart. Christian ethics reflects the creativeness of the Cross, bearing the power and the principle to solve our moral problems.

True forgiveness, which all penitent sinners receive at the Cross, at once revives and transforms them. Genuine faith in a person really means salvation, not merely a reward given with salvation. To be forgiven much (like the sinful woman described in Luke 7) is to love much, and also to live much and to live anew.

Christians live by such saving faith and work through the love that flows from the Cross. This becomes the "rose-bloom" on their faith. Indeed, Christian goodness becomes "grace goodness"—our spontaneous obedience to God's mercy toward us in Christ's cross. God not only receives us as His own, but we become infused with a power that compels us to act in love and service.

God's forgiving grace remains actually the mightiest and most permanent force in the moral world. When we know we are forgiven by God for Christ's sake, we become moved to forgive others. Our good works are truly an expression of gratitude, of praise to God.

On the cross, God in Christ not only bore our sins, but the power of His grace created new life in us. Born of the Holy Spirit, He calls us to become what we potentially are—new creatures in Christ Jesus. We who were once dead in trespasses and sins receive new life to live in obedience to God. There abides matchless regenerative power in divine forgiveness. It both calls us and compels us to be saints—holy to the Lord.

The New Testament religion has been defined as grace, and its ethics remain focused on gratitude. So P. T. Forsyth rightly amended Augustine's version, saying, "Love (as the holy and atoning cross creates love) and do what you will. That is the Christian ethic."[3]

That New Testament grace and ethic becomes both a crisis and a process. God forgives us the moment we in faith confess and repent of our sins. But divine forgiveness continues only as we forgive those who wrong us. The Christian ethic of love holds sway in our lives both because God implanted His love in our hearts and because we follow its leadings in daily living.

That love remains the Divine vitality that everywhere produces and restores life. It gives to each of us the power of working miracles—if we will. As we shall see, to truly follow the course of love which God expects from His obedient children, He calls us to total devotion and commitment. The call to be saints is a call to consecration.

Consecrated to Be Servants

Take my life, and let it be
Consecrated, Lord, to Thee.

Take my moments and my days,
Let them flow in ceaseless praise.

Take my hands, and let them move
At the impulse of Thy love.[4]

To Frances Ridley Havergal, author of "Take My Life, and Let It Be," the significance of consecration came in a flash. She testified: "It was on Advent Sunday that I first saw the blessedness of true consecration. I saw it in a flash, and what you see you can never un-see. There must be full surrender before there can be full blessedness. God admits you by one into the other."

We recall Jesus said, ". . . whoever wants to become great among you must be your servant, and whoever wants to be first must be your slave—just as the Son of Man did not come to be served, but to serve, and give his life a ransom for many" (Matt. 20:26-28).

Christ's winsome and holy life of service to God the Father and mankind become shown by His total consecration to do thy will of His Father. The Psalmist's words, "I delight to do thy will, O my God" (40:8, KJV), were what Jesus expressed throughout His life. In like menner, the measure we consecrate ourselves to God, our lives will be marked by love and service.

The root import of the word "concecration" is: "separation from a common use and solemn dedication to a sacred use." Combined are separation, a decision of human responsability; dedication, the human act of devotion; and consecration, God's acceptance of our dedication.

When we devote and dedicate our lives to God's purpose, He consecrates us to His service. True consecration ocurrs in our lives only as God enables us. As we offer ourselves to Him in faith, he works His will in us. He consecrates us to himself that He might make us holy in what we do, say, and think.

The whole question about such faith that enables the believer to gain full salvation becomes simply whether he will sell *all* to buy this "pearl of great price." Self must even give up its own right to retain a hold on all things. But the result is well worth the commitment.

A man hiking at night fell into a dry well. He cries for help eventually brought someone to him. They let down a rope and tried to haul him up, but the line kept slipping through the fallen man's hands.

Suspecting the man's grip become weak because of trying to hold on to other things besides the rope, the rescuer called out, "Do you have something in your hands?"

"Yes," replied the man—after a pause, "I have some parcels I want to save as well as myself." He could not muster enough strength in his hands to hold fast to the rope until he gave up his parcels.[6] His struggle reflects the inner choice a person must make to enjoy Christian living.

No one automatically grows into consecration—it is by choice, not chance. The apostle Paul exhorts: "I urge you, . . . in view of God's mercy, to offer yourselves as living sacrifices, holy and pleasing to God—which is your spiritual act of worship" (Rom. 12:1).

No positive Christian practice happens without basic Christian experience. The Divine order is first, principle, then practice; first, doctrine, then duty; first revelation, then responsibility. God's truth must be first known and obeyed in basic experience to produce a real, fruitful beyond our own doing. God fills the person who loves His precepts with an enabling Presence. Paul said, "It is not I, but Christ living in me" (cf. Gal. 2:20).

A consecrated life is one dedicated to doing the will of God. One has suggested that in consecration a person brings his life to God as a blank sheet of paper, signing his name at the bottom, and giving it to the Heavenly Father. Trusting His love, we invite Him to fill in the details. With such a commitment, Paul declares we will "be able to test and approve what God's will is—his good, pleasing and perfect will" (Rom. 12:2).

Madam Guyon once said, "God will give us opportunity to try our consecration, whether it be a true one or not. No man can be wholly the Lord's unless he is wholly consecrated to the Lord; and no man can know whether he is thus wholly consecrated except by tribulation. That is the test."[7]

Offering oneself as a living sacrifice becomes a spiritual transaction as well as an outward action. Rather than conform to the pattern of this world, the Apostle says, "Be transformed by the renewing of your mind" (Rom. 12:2).

Philip Henry, father of Matthew Henry who became a great Bible commentator, taught his children this prayer:[8]

> I take God the Father to be my God;
> I take God the Son to be my Savior;
> I take God the Holy Ghost to be my Sanctifier;
> I take God the Word to be my rule;
> I take people of God to be my people;
> And I do hereby dedicate and yield my whole self to the Lord;
> And I do this deliberately, freely, and forever. Amen.

To thus submit our lives to the Lord may seem like an absurd price to pay. But was not Christ's offering of himself to purchase our pardon and redemption infinitely more costly?

A missionary who had long observed the building of an ornate temple in India asked a local woman, "How much will it cost?"

"It is for the gods," she replied, "We do not ask what it will cost."

We have no excuse or right to hold back our lives from the living God because of fear of what it might cost us. Being a Christian means that in response to Jesus Christ's full offering, one yields his whole self to Him. Christ's loving sacrifice for our redemption demands no less than our all in service to Him.

Paul says, "Live a life of love, just as Christ loved us and gave himself up for us as a fragrant offering and sacrifice to God" (Eph. 5:2). Compare those words with Jesus' statement in Matt. 20:28: " . . . the Son of Man did not come to be served, but to serve, and to give his life a ransom for many."

The Apostle goes on to say, "Husbands, love your wives, just as Christ loved the church and gave himself up for her to make her holy, cleansing her by the washing with water through the word, . . . " (Eph. 5:25-26).

Again, Paul shows Christ to be our example. Paul declares: "Your attitude should be the same as that of Christ Jesus: Who being in very nature God, did not consider equality with God something to be grasped, but made himself nothing, taking the very nature of a servant, . . . " (Phil. 2:5-7).

A consecrated life becomes one separated to the glory of God. There must be a complete turning from sin if there is to be separation to God. The Apostle exhorts: "Since we have these promises, . . . let us purify ourselves from everything that contaminates body and spirit, and let us strive for perfection out of reverence for God" (2 Cor. 7:1).

Strengthened by the Holy Spirit, we can renounce everything we know to be against God by a devoted act of our renewed wills. "It is God who works in you to will and do what pleases him" (Phil. 2:13). The Christian becomes insulated from what is sinful rather than isolated from it.

A consecrated Christian must go on living in an evil world among sinful people. He hates the wicked display, but he has a passion for the right and works for the glory of God and Christ. The Christian tests all his actions by the standard: "Is this for the glory of God?" One totally consecrated will do anything, surrender anything, suffer anything, if only God becomes glorified.

Nothing is too costly to give to the Lord as Master. The watchword of Christian devotion becomes: "I will do it for Jesus' sake!" Sacrifice has been described as the ecstasy of giving the best we have to the One we love the most.

The consecrated life also becomes concentrated on the service of God. A convert testified that the Lord had helped him along the line of consecration. But he didn't use the correct word. He said it two or three times like this: "I'm so glad He helped me to be wholly *concentrated* unto Him." That growing Christian may have used the wrong word, but he expressed the right idea.

Consecration will always concentrate on God and His service. The act is not an end in itself. If consecration isn't expressed in holy action, it becomes a sham. The truly consecrated Christian will say with the Apostle, "But one thing I do: Forgetting what is behind and straining toward what is ahead, I press on toward the goal to win the prize for which God has called me heavenward in Christ Jesus" (Phil. 3:13-14).

Our motives should involve the knowledge that we become saved to proclaim eternal life to a world estranged from God. The Lord sends us to devote ourselves without reserve to that sacred task. Jesus said to His followers: "As the Father has sent me, I am sending you" (John 20:21). As the Father sent the Son from heaven to be the Savior of the world, the Son sends us to be His evangels throughout the world.

The public form of love is righteousness. Truly Christian love cannot be severed from righteousness, which is "applied holiness" within one's personal life. The Christian attitude to social, economic, political, and international issues becomes shaped by the Cross. In every realm of human relations Christian love will demand social justice, fair exchange, honest government, and peaceful national goals.

God wants nothing less than our total commitment to carry His words of hope into this sin-scarred world. We become chosen vessels for His holy purpose in making salvation known. The perfect holiness of God remains the ground of the Christian religion. Even the Lord's Prayer, which says, "Hallowed by your name" (Matt. 6:9), defines concepts of the love of God.

But love "is not evangelical till it has dealt with holy law. In the midst of the rainbow there is a throne."[9]

Sanctification and Cleansing

The distance that mankind fell becomes regained through faith in a Redeemer to come. Forgiveness became first offered through the symbols of the slain lamb and the burning altar. Believers stood accounted as righteous and holy unto the Lord. A quality of divine favor became restored to them. But with the coming of Jesus Christ, those who accepted and believed in Him became actual "partakers of his holiness" (Heb. 12:10, KJV). The Word declares that through Jesus' atoning blood, mankind's lost relationship with the Father can be recovered.

Before Adam's fall, he had holy communion with the Heavenly Father of all creation. But with mankind's revolt, evil entered and marred the sacred fellowship. The holy bond of fellowship became broken. All mankind lost the godly character with which they were first created.

God acted to provide forgiveness and new life for the human race dead in trespasses and sins, to restore that holy divine-human relationship. This becomes a step toward the desired end, but not the end itself. When a person confesses and repents of his sin, receiving pardon and new birth, he begins to walk in God's way. But God has purchased also the full cleansing of our lives with the blood of His Son.

The apostle Peter says God commands that we be like Him: "Be holy, because I am holy" (1 Pet. 1:16; cf. Lev. 11:44-45). The Father wants His children to be cleansed and made holy. They should enter His holy dwelling and abide with Him forevermore. Whoever comes to Him in faith, He will apply the blood of His Son, cleanse them from their wicked ways, and receive them into His holy, blameless family.

Scripture further declares Jesus Christ "is able to save completely those who come to God through him, because he always lives to intercede for them" (Heb. 7:25). The "uttermost" to which God can lift a depraved and deprived person cannot be less than that degree of heart purity given mankind when He first created Adam. Since the race was holy in the beginning, He is able to restore it to that same degree of holiness. Individuals become required to fully submit to God and by faith commit themselves to His will.

God calls us to true personal holiness here and now. The apostle Paul writes: "For God did not call us to be impure, but to live a holy life. Therefore, he who rejects this instruction does not reject man but God, who gives you his Holy Spirit" (1 Thess. 4:7-8).

Since Paul obviously writes to a church of regenerated believers, some degree of uncleanness must have lurked in their hearts. "Uncleanness" and "holiness" are in contrast. When one becomes sanctified, made holy, he becomes purified from selfish pride that tends to go against God. The believer becomes cleansed from an evil temper that would defile, and from a disposition that rules in resentment.

The Apostle further says, "Christ loved the church and gave himself up for her to make her holy, cleansing her by the washing with water through the word, and to present her to himself as a radiant church, without stain or wrinkle or any other blemish, but holy and blameless" (Eph. 5:25-27).

Christ's boundless love, the holy purpose and purchase price to which He gave himself to sanctify and cleanse His church, likewise demands our all. Those called by His holy name cannot risk resisting His full claim on their lives. His Spirit's cleansing enables complete loving obedience to His will and way, providing a holy inheritance for His people.

Charles G. Finney, 19th century evangelist, described his experience as he responded to the Holy Spirit's leading. He said: "As I turned to take a seat by the fire, I received the mighty baptism of the Holy Spirit. The Holy Ghost descended upon me in a manner that seemed to go through me, body and soul. I could feel the impressions like a wave of electricity going through and through me. Indeed, it seemed to come in waves and waves of liquid love; for I could not express it any other way. I wept aloud with joy and love . . . ."[10]

In his writing, Finney declares, "He who neglects to obey the command to be filled with the Spirit is as guilty of breaking the command of God, as he who steals, or curses, or commits adultery. His guilt is as great as the authority of God is great, who commands us to be filled. His guilt is equivalent to all the good he might do if he were filled with the Spirit."[11]

Once called out of sin, and claiming Christ's forgiving grace, we must not cling to the old corruption that filled the hearts of those who slew Him. The bruises, the five wounds, and bloodstains of our Savior bid our commitment to His loving holiness. "Jesus also suffered outside the city gate to make his people holy through his own blood" (Heb. 13:12).

Christ died to provide sanctification for believers as well as to offer the sacrifice for forgiveness of sin. He paid the price that Adam's race might be lifted out of the mire of sin and regain a holy relationship with God. Jesus provides the "holiness, without which no man shall see the Lord" (Heb. 12:14, KJV). The proof that we have the baptism with the Holy Spirit is that we bear a family likeness to Jesus Christ. People should take knowledge of us, as they did of the disciples, that we have been with Jesus.[12]

Our sanctification is the fruition of the Spirit-implanted life whereas before we were dead in transgressions and sins (Eph. 2:1). The Holy Spirit infills and cleanses as we yield our lives to His control. But our personal holiness depends on the merits of Jesus' atoning sacrifice. Through Him we receive forgiveness and new life, full salvation, which includes freedom from the moral defilement of inbred sin.

That forgiving grace must be exercised to employ growth in grace. Any growth in the love of God manifested in Christ Jesus occurs by our pleading His blood shed on our behalf. We are both forgiven and justified before God, cleansed and made holy because of our Lord working through the Holy Spirit.

The Spirit applies Jesus' sacrifice to our hearts and lives so we may fully obey Him in truth and love. We desire to do His will rather than follow selfish whims. we become led to forgive as we have been forgiven. The blood of Jesus Christ continues to cleanse us from all sin (1 John 1:7) only as we maintain a heart that forgives those who wrong us.

The Holy Spirit brings one inner peace and a sense of freedom from condemnation (Rom. 8:1). "Therefore, since we have been justified through faith, we have peace with God through our Lord Jesus Christ"

(Rom. 5:1). The Spirit removes the old guilty effects of enmity against God and gives witness that we belong to God's family. "For you did not receive a spirit that makes you a slave again to fear, but you received the Spirit who makes you sons. And by him we cry, 'Abba, Father.' The Spirit himself testifies with our spirit that we are God's children" (Rom. 8:15-16).

John Wesley described his heart-warming experience, saying, "I felt I did trust in Christ, in Christ alone for my salvation; and an assurance was given me, that he had taken away my sins, even mine, and saved me from the law of sin and death."[13]

The ability to do right remains no longer a sterile abstraction. The impulse of conscience has been reinforced by the cleansing power of Christ's atonement. One now delights to obey the law because he loves the Lawgiver. His affections are purified, withdrawn from all unworthy objects, and centered on Jesus Christ. The believer's will, the core of his personality, once the stronghold of rebellion, becomes fused into the will of Christ, melded in the furnace of His mighty love.

Jesus Christ's atoning work for our justification and the indwelling of His Spirit for our sanctification astounds our understanding. We wonder in what sense we can be made holy in heart by the shedding of Jesus' blood. In God's Word, sin (distinguished from sins and sinning) is described as a spiritual entity, e.g., "the body of sin" (Rom. 6:6), "the sinful mind" (Rom. 8:7), and "sinful nature" (Rom. 7:17).

The essential purpose of sanctification is to do away with that condemning entity. Sanctification refers to a moral cleansing of our nature from its defiling presence and power, removing inner depravity, and bringing healing to the soul. A clearer understanding of how we are made holy by the blood of Christ occurs by the use of figurative language.

Thomas Cook once wrote:

> When we speak of the blood of Jesus cleansing from sin, we do not mean that the blood of Christ is literally applied to the heart. What is meant is that through the great atoning work Christ has . . . purchased complete deliverance from sin for us exactly as He has made forgiveness possible for us. But while Christ is thus through

His death what may be called the procuring cause of sanctification, the work itself is wrought in us through the agency of the Holy Spirit. He comes to the heart in sanctifying power, excluding the evil and filling it with love (when we believe the blood cleanseth us from all sin), just as He comes in regenerating power when we believe for forgiveness and are adopted into the family of God.[14]

The apostle Paul sets forth the scope of our redemption: "Christ redeemed us from the curse of the law by becoming a curse for us, . . . so that by faith we might receive the promise of the Spirit" (Gal. 3:13-14). Again, Paul says Christ "gave himself for us to redeem us from all wickedness and to purify for himself a people that are his very own, eager to do what is good" (Titus 2:14). The future glory includes "the redemption of our bodies" (Rom. 8:23).

A believer's deliverance exceeds a mere negation of sin—it becomes a positive estate. The price Jesus Christ paid for our freedom from sin has purchased for us a spiritual power that can keep us from ever falling under the curse again—through the gift of the Holy Spirit. Because Jesus shed His precious blood, we may receive the fullness of His Spirit. Our lives, once so darkened by the curse and stained with sin, become His temple and home. We experience "an indwelling God."[15]

Jesus's atoning blood frees us from indwelling sin by cleansing that rebel nature. As Christ's abiding Spirit infills us, He kindles within us a zeal for holy living—unto every good work. This, then, becomes redemption's full result, purity of heart, and possessed by God to follow His love. We live before others and serve God as mature persons.

In a letter to the Bishop of London, answering the question, "What is meant by one who is perfect?" John Wesley says:

> We mean one in whom is "the mind which was in Christ," and who so "walked as He walked;" a man that "hath clean hands and a pure heart," or that is "cleansed from all filthiness of flesh and spirit" . . . one whom God hath sanctified throughout, even in "body, soul, and spirit;" one who "walketh in the light as He is in the light, in whom is no darkness at all," the blood of Jesus Christ His Son, "having

cleansed him from all sin." . . . He is holy as God who called him is holy, both in life and "in all manner of conversation." He "loveth the Lord his God with all his heart, and serveth him with all his strength." He loveth his neighbor (every man) as himself, yea, "as Christ loved us"—them in particular that "despitefully use him and persecute him."[16]

God has a holy ideal for every person's life. This divine purpose involves God's highest glory and our greatest good. God gave the Holy Spirit to lead believers from the cradle to the grave—and beyond. We attain life's true goals as we follow our divine Guide. Christians who walk maturely in the light of truth realize the blood of Jesus Christ cleanses from all sin, both actual and original.

The frequent questions raised about the Spirit's clear guidance miss truly knowing His wise and loving movements in all the details of life. Rather, the issue rests in our total and continual abandonment of selfishness to enthrone Christ within. Once this matter is settled, our adjustment to God's holy will becomes a happy way. We become reconciled unto God.

NOTES

1. W. T. Purkiser, "The Two Meanings of Grace," *Herald of Holiness*, May 21, 1975, 18.

2. William M. Greathouse, *The Fullness of the Spirit* (Kansas City: Nazarene Publishing House, 1958), 11.

3. P. T. Forsyth, *The Christian Ethic of War* (New York: Longman's, Green, 1917), 137.

4. Frances Ridley Havergal, *Kept for the Master's Use* (Chicago: Donohue, Henneberry & Co., 1879), flyleaf.

5. J. Oswald Sanders, *Cultivation of Christian Character* (Chicago: Moody Press, 1965), 23.

6. Cited in Daniel Steele, *Hints for Holy Living* (Kansas City: Beacon Hill Press, 1959), 25.

7. Cited in John Gregory Mantle, *Beyond Humiliation* (Chicago: Moody Press, n.d.), 221.

8. Cited in J. Oswald Sanders, *Cultivation of Christian Character*, 24.

9. P. T. Forsyth, *God the Holy Father*, 5.

10. Walter B. Knight, *Master Book of New Illustrations*, 217.

11. Ibid.

12. Oswald Chambers, *Conformed to His Image*, 58.

13. John Wesley, *Works*, I, 103.

14. Cited in A. Paget Wilkes, *Dynamic of Redemption*, 77.

15. Cf. Ibid., 86-87.

16. John Wesley, *Works*, VIII, 484, 485.

CHAPTER

IX

Our Ministry of Reconciliation

The third article of faith in the Apostles' Creed declares: "I believe in the Holy Ghost, the holy Church of Jesus Christ, the communion of saints, the forgiveness of sins, . . . "

The Church, the Body of Christ, became born of the Holy Spirit and quickened to enhance individual lives by the gifts of the Spirit. Divine creation, mankind's fellowship with God, the fullness of redemption, and new life in Christ's kingdom become applied in personal experience. All individual Christian service and joint work of the Church gain final meaning through the Holy Spirit's sanctifying action.

The New Testament book of the Acts of the Apostles could be titled, "The Acts of the Holy Spirit in and Through the Apostles." Receiving the Holy Spirit, the Early Church experienced the abiding presence of the God who made heaven and earth, who became incarnate in Jesus Christ. The Spirit, Giver of life and power, revealed "God in Christ" to be the Savior of mankind, not only in name but in deed.

Without the work of the Holy Spirit, Jesus' crucifixion and resurrection would have been only hollow historical events. The coming of the Spirit made genuine witnessing possible. Jesus told His disciples, "But you will receive power when the Holy Spirit comes on you; and you will be my witnesses in Jerusalem, and in all Judea and Samaria, and to the ends of the earth" (Acts 1:8).

Arming the disciples with the fullness of His promise, the ascended Lord sent the Holy Spirit at Pentecost, and the mission of the Christ began. As His witnesses, the Church proclaimed the gospel of reconciliation, the forgiveness of confessed sins, and the glory of restored relationships through the power of Christ's Spirit.

The New Testament variously refers to the Holy Spirit as "the Spirit of Jesus" (Acts 16:6-7), "the Spirit of Christ" (Rom. 8:9), and "the Spirit of the Son" (Gal. 4:6). John applies the special title of the Holy Spirit, the Paraclete (advocate), to Jesus himself: "We have an advocate with the Father, Jesus Christ the righteous" (1 John 2:1, KJV). Paul says, "The Lord [meaning Christ] is the Spirit" (2 Cor. 3:17).

From our viewpoint, little distinction can be made between Christ and the Spirit. Objectively they are different, for Scripture doesn't identify the person of the Holy Spirit with the person of Christ. But subjectively they are the same. We don't experience the presence of the Spirit instead of the presence of Christ. Rather, the indwelling Spirit is the indwelling Christ. The Apostle says, "If anyone does not have the Spirit of Christ, he does not belong to Christ" (Rom. 8:9b).

Though the Holy Spirit is Christ's present agent on earth, He is like the wind. He remains sovereign to do as He please, just as the wind blows where it lists. The Spirit is present in mystery and power, but we cannot chart His course. Jesus told Nicodemus: "The wind blows wherever it pleases. You may hear its sound, but you cannot tell where it comes from or where it is going. So it is with everyone born of the Spirit" (John 3:8).

The Holy Spirit did not use the same method or manner with Peter, Paul, or John in New Testament times. Nor did He deal the same with such church fathers as Clement, Origen, and Polycarp. The Spirit did not work in the Reformation as He did in the Great Awakening. He used Savonarola, Knox, Luther, and Wycliffe differently than Wesley, Whitefield, and Moody. Nor does the Holy Spirit move the same in revivals today as He did in the Awakening. But His holy purpose and guidance remain constant to those who receive Him.

The Holy Spirit works according to *kairos* time, "the right time," and in personal challenge. T. A. Kantonene rightly declares, "To become a Christian is as individual a matter as to be born."[1] It does not occur as a social or family inheritance. Even one born into a Christian home or community must deal with the edict: "You must be born again." This new birth becomes a matter of life, not merely of belief or tradition, code, or institution.

Being a Christian means more than to know and accept what the Church teaches. Also it means more than to join and work for the growth of the Church, or to conform to Christian standards of conduct. One must die to self and be made alive in Christ, born into the new life that began with His death and resurrection.

This new life is not the outgrowth of our own religious aspirations. It becomes planted in our hearts by the life-bearing gospel seed that is the power of God unto salvation. Paul says, "Faith comes from hearing the message, and the message is heard through the word of Christ" (Rom. 10:17). God's will to save people becomes realized only as we truly believe redemption is in Christ Jesus.

Faith is a trustful response that allows God to have full sway in one's life. It becomes a life standpoint of God-centeredness, just as sin is a life attitude of self-centeredness. As Kierkegaard suggests, faith becomes a double movement of eternity, God's movement to us in grace and our movement to Him in surrender.

The doctrine of regeneration leads to entire sanctification as naturally as birth leads to growth. Regeneration is not an end in itself. It signals only the beginning of new life in the Spirit. Without the new birth there is no new life. Without growth the new life becomes lost, and reconciliation between God and mankind and among people becomes squelched.

Sadhu Sundar Singh, and Indian Sikh, became torn between his old religion and Christianity. He spent a night in reading, meditation and prayer. Just before the new day dawned, a bright cloud filled the room. In the cloud he saw the radiant figure of Jesus Christ. It seemed to him Jesus said: "Why do you oppose Me? I am your Savior; I died on the cross for you." From that time on Sundar Singh became a devoted follower of Christ.[2]

Such a vision doesn't occur at every conversion experience. But a real miracle transports the penitent heart from spiritual darkness and death into the light and life of forgiveness. The second great step of faith is a further work of divine grace, distinct and witnessed to by the operation of the Holy Spirit on the believer's consciousness. It occurs as clearly witnessed by the Spirit as the new birth.

Our return to the favor of God includes a degree of cleansing. All committed sins become graciously forgiven, and their pollution becomes largely purged away. To an extent, one is made holy when he becomes born again, but he is not sanctified wholly. That awaits the total yielding of oneself to God, for Him to possess and guide as He wills.

As we trust the Holy Spirit, He infills us to cleanse the depraved sinful nature. We receive divine witness when our consecration and cleansing becomes complete, for our wandering and divided hearts are fully reconciled unto God. Joy attends our conscious knowledge that God's pardon and cleansing has transformed our sin-plagued lives. Jesus Christ has become truly Lord of our lives.

This life-cleansing brings peace which the world cannot give—nor take away. Jesus tells His followers: "Peace I leave with you; my peace I give to you . . . ." (John 14:27).

At Peace With God and Mankind

A psychiatrist once declared, "With Peace in his soul a man can face the most terrifying experiences. But without peace in his soul he cannot manage even as simple a task as writing a letter."

How important is our peace with God! Our interpersonal relationships depend on our terms with Him. Though once rebels and outcasts, we may by faith unite with God's holy kingdom and purpose. We must allow His spirit to direct our lives. The author of Hebrews writes: "Make level paths for your feet, so that the lame may not be disabled, but rather healed. Make every effort to live in peace with all men and to be holy; without holiness no one will see the Lord" (12:13-14).

This scripture includes our ministry of reconciliation toward our neighbors along with holy union in God's will. Living in peace with others becomes the secret of being holy before the Lord. God requires the holiness one receives when he is wholly sanctified, when his heart is filled with perfect love. Such love is divine and self-sacrificing. It forsakes selfish goals to rescue others and to glorify God.

Many believers have grasped the rich, strong words: "And the peace of God which transcends all understanding will guard your hearts and your minds in Christ Jesus" (Phil. 4:7). God's peace for us through Christ acts as an armed guard drawn up around our hearts and thoughts to repel unrest. It stands beyond intellectual analysis, but His peace surrounds and steadies the trusting heart. Paul prays: "May God himself, the God of peace, sanctify you through and through. May your whole spirit, soul and body be kept blameless at the coming of our Lord Jesus Christ" (1 Thess. 5:23).

One cannot understand such an experience, but he can feel God's peace. Though a person cannot grasp it with head knowledge, he can possess the assurance of faith. In a sense, the believer does not get this peace—it is given by God to embrace him. When a person becomes justified by faith, he seeks and finds a new order in life. He is now "in Christ." This "new birth" occurs by "looking unto Jesus the author and finisher of our faith" (Heb. 12:2, KJV). Following Christ, we both look a new direction, and we obtain power to live a victorious life.

The converted sinner, rather than gazing inward, looks outward—not trusting any supposed merit in himself. He centers on the love and grace of an absolutely trustworthy God. The redeemed do not look downward, but upward. "Looking unto Jesus" means looking away from sin's alluring shame, up to the beauty and purity of Christ.

Also, the believer begins looking forward, not backward. He joins the Apostle in saying, "Forgetting what is behind and straining toward what is ahead, I press on toward the goal to win the prize for which God has called me heavenward in Christ Jesus" (Phil. 3:13-14).

The sanctified life has been viewed as a secondary work of the Holy

Spirit, superimposed on the original divine act of justification as an added extra. God really intends no such gap. Justification carries life with it. Those who confess and repent of their sins, and by faith accept Christ as their Savior, find life. The righteousness of God into which a Christian enters by faith becomes not merely an uprightness God demands or confers, but also a righteousness God refines.

Entire sanctification is not a new idea. As James Stewart suggests, it is the Holy Spirit unfolding in us a life-force already present. In a sense, God's justifying verdict itself sanctifies, making the sinful heart holy.[3] It makes one a new creature and seeks to purify the heart to live blameless before God. It translates a person's soul from the domain of the flesh and evil spirits into the control of Christ's Spirit.

Even a justified person walks straight and lives clean, in his right mind before God. Receiving justifying grace and forgiveness by faith prepares the believer to live a sanctified life. The experience of the two religious crises are in the process of divine leading and purpose. A distinction becomes noted because of sinful acts and the nature of sin one's faith in Christ must conquer separately.

Jesus accepted sinners during His ministry on earth, without any sign of merit. Somehow their confession of faith in Him brought about its own proof. Christ's forgiveness not only canceled the past, but brought them new life in the present, and made them saints for the future. Divine love and trust became placed on those who thought they had forfeited all such love and trust forever.

God transforms the present and future of any poor lost sinner, who has nothing to offer but the cry, "Lord, save me, or I perish." He banks on Jesus' cry from the cross, "It is finished!" God gladly accepts the risk for Jesus' sake and justifies the penitent sinner. True faith becomes verified by a transformed life that once seemed impossible.

This is the scriptural link between justification and sanctification. The Divine love that takes life's greatest risks also creates life's most glorious results. God waits for no human guarantees, but fully pardons when we confess our need. He dares to trust those who have no right or claim for trust at all. God's forgiveness renews ever penitent heart, and His justification occurs to sanctify.

Christ purposed to create in himself one new human being, making peace between the children of the covenant and those without hope. "He came and preached peace to you who were far away and peace to those who were near. For through him we both have access to the Father by one Spirit" (Eph. 2:17-18).

Paul outlines the holy action in one's personal redeeming experience. The forgiven person becomes possessed by a power greater than his own. The Apostle declares the change comes through the truth in Jesus. "You were taught, with regard to your former way of life, to put off your old self, which is being corrupted by its deceitful desires; to be made new in the attitude of your minds; and to put on the new self, created to be like God in true righteousness and holiness" (Eph. 4:21b-23).

This new life from God creates results that once could not have happened. The fresh spiritual status bears fruit daily. Our identification with Christ means we "are being transformed into his likeness with ever-increasing glory, which comes from the Lord, who is the Spirit" (2 Cor. 3:18).

The steady light of divine love shines in lives once darkened by sin. From that love also flows the energy to do holy deeds. The Lord's holy kiss of forgiveness plants hope where ever-increasing despair once prevailed. Now rises the victor's shout, "I can do all things through Him who strengthens me" (Phil. 4:13, NASB).

Paul proclaims our salvation has a bright and lasting hope. "Therefore, since we have been justified through faith, we have peace with God through our Lord Jesus Christ, through whom we have gained access by faith into this grace in which we now stand. And we rejoice in the hope of the glory of God" (Rom. 5:1-2). The Apostle further declares, "For we through the Spirit, by faith, are waiting for the hope of righteousness" (Gal. 5:5, NASB).

God's justifying decree, received at one's conversion, now anticipates the happy verdict of the final judgment. Since there awaits "no condemnation" to those who are in Christ Jesus, who walk in the

Spirit (Rom. 8:1), all such converts can know the fullness of divine salvation. The age of the Holy Spirit truly begins as He indwells believers, cleansing from all sin and filling their hearts with God's love. When Christians fully consecrate themselves they enter a new realm of joy and freedom through the healing of divine and human relationships.

The gift of the Holy Spirit becomes a foretaste of our total redemption (Rom. 8:23). We receive His "seal of ownership" (2 Cor. 1:22), waiting for the time when Christ will return in glory. And we will appear with Him (Col. 3:4) as citizens of heaven, reconciled unto God. Our crucial pilgrimage began when we were dead in trespasses and sins. It progressed as we became raised to new life, to become holy as God is holy.

The Word of Reconciliation

Italian reformer Girolamo Savonarola stood as a lone prophet of righteousness in Florence, a city whose corruption caused an appalling scenario. Yet because he faithfully preached the gospel truth, an incredible change took place. A historian reports the total aspect of the city became altered. The women forsook their lavish jewels and finery, dressed plainly, and bore themselves demurely. Lawless your Florentines became transformed as by magic into sober, religious men.

Pious hymns took the place of Lorenzo's carnival songs. Bankers and tradesmen became impelled by "scruples of conscience" to restore ill-gotten gains, "amounting to many thousand flourins." People threw away their evil books and lewd pictures, and on the last day of the 1497 carnival they piled all these materials in the great square and burned it in a bonfire to the glory of God.[4]

The Word of reconciliation resounded with power from Savonarola, as it does from the lips of all faithful men and women. A wonderful change takes place within any society and among individuals when the Divine message becomes received. God's Word will not return to Him empty.

Paul repeatedly declares God's salvation becomes revealed through reconciliation. Our settled relationship comes through a transformed life. "If any man is in Christ, he is a new creature; the old things passed away;

behold new things have come" (2 Cor. 5:17, NASB). The Apostle says all these things come from God, who reconciled us to himself through Christ, and entrusts us with the ministry of reconciliation (v. 18). "God was in Christ reconciling the world to Himself, no counting their trespasses against them, and He has committed to us the word of reconciliation" (v. 19, NASB).

God requires our restoration to His life and service before we can have restored fellowship with others. Selfish concern must be transformed, changed and uplifted to have regard for the welfare of those outside the household of faith. It also seeks right relations with fellow Christians.

The ministry of reconciliation demands the Divine act centered in "the word of reconciliation." This word becomes more than a message, it is a forgiving act induced by the Holy Spirit, moving believers to pardon those who have wronged them, as God for Christ's sake has forgiven them. Just as sin sets person against person, the forgiveness of sin in Christ unites mankind into a redeemed fellowship—the Church.

The Church is not simply a community of forgiven believers in Christ. But the people of God become joined in the action of preaching and forgiving. As Martin Luther suggests, the work of the church is to show the world the "togetherness of hearts in the faith." This unites into one body those who believe in Christ, and who allow His Holy Spirit to control their personal and corporate lives.

Our unity as Christians is an accomplished fact. Despite various backgrounds, the Holy Spirit draws believers together. The Apostle declares, all who have been baptized into Christ form one body (1 Cor. 12:12-13). We have been sealed by God's saving grace in Christ and by the gift of the Holy Spirit to indwell our lives.

P. T. Fosyth, in his book *Church and Sacraments*, says there is but one sacrament. It is the Word, the gospel of God's grace in Christ. It can be conveyed either by preaching or by a formal sacred act. So the Bible, properly used, becomes "the sacramental book" by the Holy Spirit's action through inspiration and revelation.[5]

Forsyth further explains the sacraments are "the acted Word, variants of the preached Word." Though they remain signs, they are the Word itself, visible, as the Word becomes audible in true preaching. Either as a sign or as the Word, a sacrament is an act. It is the real presence of Christ giving us His redemption anew, meeting life's deepest needs. The Master's forgiving and healing acts become present by the Holy Spirit's enabling power in the Church.[6]

The word of reconciliation is thus an act. It is both spoken and offered as new life in Christ. A change takes place, both in standing and relationship before God. Through Jesus' sacrificial death and resurrected life, we by faith receive new life—justified, reconciled unto God. Divine pardon redeems us from sin unto righteousness. We become born again, by the Spirit, to receive His holy enabling. Our obedience to God is the response of the reconciled to the Reconciler.

The New Testament presents God as the subject, never the object of any reconciling to be done. Paul declared, "We are therefore Christ's ambassadors, as though God were making his appeal through us. We implore you on Christ's behalf: Be reconciled to God" (2 Cor. 5:20). This is Christianity's distinctive glory and challenge in every age, in every generation, in the life of every believer.

Everything that concerns our salvation starts from God's side. Even faith, penitence, and prayer, heart attitudes that might appear to originate in mankind as human virtues, are of God's creation. Faith is God's gift because it becomes evoked by the revelation of himself as worthy of our total trust. God prompted penitence because it becomes produced by that reaction to sin which culminated on the Cross. Prayer also comes from God because when "we do not know how we ought to pray, . . . the Spirit himself intercedes for us . . . " (Rom. 8:26).

Baron von Hugel once wrote to a niece, "The passion and hunger for God comes from God, and God answers it with Christ."[7] Over the greatest moral and spiritual triumphs of this life the saints can only cry with the Psalmist: "Not to us, O Lord, not to us but to your name be the glory, because of your love and faithfulness" (Psa. 115:1).

Surprisingly, Jesus told His disciples, "the Son can do nothing by himself; . . . For the Father loves the Son and shows him all he does" (John

5:19-20). Then in the parable of the vine and the branches, Christ told His followers, "apart from me you can do nothing" (John 15:5).

We can do nothing of ourselves; there is no Creator but God. All moral virtue springs from Him. James S. Stewart observes:[8]

> And every virtue we possess,
> And every victory won,
> And every thought of holiness,
> Are His alone.

This defines the very meaning of divine grace and reflects the secret of reconciliation. James Moffatt says grace (*charis*) is one of the shining words that serve the world. But it is not likely that a gospel aimed to destroy human pride will ever be popular with those who bask in their own enlightenment or who trust in their own initiative for world peace. People have difficulty in properly defining between rightful self-esteem and sinful selfish pride.

Amazingly, the holy God provides for us unworthy creatures. Karl Barth points out, "Only when grace is recognized to be incomprehensible is to grace." Paul says the reality of God's salvation began for him when he ceased to struggle for divine favor, and became content to accept by faith the gift he could never win. "It is all the doing of the God who has reconciled me to Himself through Christ" (2 Cor. 5:18, Moffatt).[9]

The "word of reconciliation" becomes more powerful than the condemnation of sin. As we accept the love of Christ into our minds and hearts, old selfish pride becomes humbled; evil temper becomes purified; and resentment becomes cleansed away. The refining process begins when we confess, repent of our sins and receive divine forgiveness.

Pardon comes as a holy kiss because it constrains us to abide in God's redeeming love. We cease the habits of sin and seek deliverance from the nature that rebels against God. His Holy Spirit leads us to be filled with the cleansing love of His holy presence. We become enabled to do His will and unite with believers in a forgiving fellowship. Our union becomes bound in faith and love for each other. It is a sacred tie that binds us closer than other earthly bonds of relationship.

NOTES

1. T. A. Kantonen, *Theology of Evangelism* (Philadelphia: Muhlenberg Press, 1954), 79.
2. A. Gordon Nasby (ed.), *1041 Sermon Illustrations, Ideas, and Expositions*, 69-70.
3. James S. Stewart, *A Man in Christ*, 258.
4. Cited in Nasby (ed.), *1041 Sermon Illustrations, Ideas, and Expositions*, 373-374; cf. Ralph Roeder, *The Man of the Renaissance* (New York: Viking Press, 1938), 70-79.
5. P. T. Forsyth, *Church and Sacraments*, 165.
6. Cf. Ibid.
7. Cited in James S. Stewart, *A Man in Christ*, 222.
8. Ibid., 223.
9. Cited in Ibid., 224.
10. T. A. Kantonen, *Theology of Evangelism*, 86.
11. Eleanor L. Doan (comp.) *431 Quotes From the Notes of Henrietta C. Mears* (Glendale, Calif.: Regal Books, 1970), 100.
12. *Hymnal of the Methodist Episcopal Church*, 492.

CHAPTER

X

Forgiveness Heals the Hopeless

I remember how Mother's tender kiss upon my bruised forehead, cut finger, or scraped knee relieved the pain. Just her care and presence made me feel the hurt would be better soon. The healing power of a mother's love often becomes compared to that of God's boundless love.

Though God's perfect holiness excuses no sin, His love forgives all sin through Jesus Christ. We have often heard, "God helps those who help themselves." But in fact, God helps those who cannot help themselves. This is why He sent His Son, Jesus, into this world. Mankind so desperately needed a Savior to deliver them from sinful destruction.

Viewing the Savior's work as an ongoing process, Jesus Christ surpasses any historical figure whose teachings we should accept and whose example we should follow. The Holy Spirit reveals Him as the living and life-changing Christ. Jesus came to bring the sin-bound victims the powerful healing of pardon, to regenerate, to redeem, and to reconcile them with God.

Some years ago, while speaking at Harvard University of Jesus Christ, Dr. Wilfred Grenfell declared, "Just as I have seen the temperature fall and life restored as some treatment benefits a dying man, so have I seen the cruel man made kind, and the drunken man made sober, and the impure man made pure, and the feeble man made strong, and the coward made brave."[1]

The Savior has set up His kingdom and continually extends it through forgiveness. As the One who forgives, Jesus conquers His enemies, He restores penitent rebels, and binds His friends to himself. Christ offers total healing for the besetting disease of sin. The besieged become released; the guilty become forgiven and receive everlasting life in Him.

The holy, loving kiss of forgiveness remains the antidote for all moral evil. God intends the world to be cured of sin by it. Through Christ's forgiving love, preached and shown in the lives of His disciples, the world becomes convinced of God's love. When sinful people see Christians loving and forgiving as Jesus did, they realize the gospel offers them hope in this life and the hereafter.

Some may question the forgiveness of others. Every believer must allow his heart to be filled with the love of Christ. A heart full of love finds it blessed to forgive, concerned to love other Christians, and possible to even love enemies. When tempted to withhold forgiveness, we recall that its healing balm affects both the forgiver and the forgiven.

Since God reveals and requires forgiveness through Jesus Christ, He also empowers us to forgive. The same God who bestows to sinners the joy of sins forgiven also leads to the fuller blessing, the inner joy of forgiving others as one has been forgiven. Christ wants to so fill us with His Spirit that by faith in the power of His love we are enabled to forgive.

Peter had asked the Master hopefully, "Is it enough to forgive an offending brother seven times?" Jesus replied, "Not seven times, but seventy times seven!" There is no "enough" with God (cf. Matt. 18:21f.). The seeming impossible becomes possible through divine love and grace working in us.

It isn't that God simply forgives us on an exchange basis. Our forgiveness of others is not a condition of His forgiveness of us. Rather, it enables us to receive God's forgiveness. We can surround our hearts with an unforgiving spirit and block the mercy and pardon of God. A wrong spirit toward another person may or may not hurt him, but it will destroy my own soul. It soon severs my saving relationship with God. Booker T. Washington discerned the case when he said, "I will not permit any man to narrow and degrade my soul by making me hate him."

In a scene from the old TV comedy of "Amos and Andy," there was a big man who would whack Andy across the chest whenever they met. Andy finally took enough of it and told Amos, "I'm fixed for him. I put a stick of dynamite in my vest pocket, and the next time he whacks me, he's going to get his hand blown off." Andy had forgotten that at the same time his own heart would be shattered.

When we court the dynamite of hatred it becomes fused to crush our own hearts as well as blast the offender. No wonder Jesus taught His disciples to pray, "Forgive us our debts, as we also have forgiven our debtors" (Matt. 6:12). He backed this prayer with the pointed comment: "But if you do not forgive men their sins, your Father will not forgive your sins" (v. 15).

The words "forgiving" and "forgiven" thus become joined in healing. Salvation cannot occur if a person separates them. Such healing and redemption come at great cost. God's holy love and grace become revealed in Christ's death and resurrection. The triumph of divine forgiveness provides the means of our reprieve from death. To really forgive means more than a surface gesture, or vocal assent. It becomes a wholehearted act that affects at least two parties.

Forgiveness Transcends Tolerance

No one truly forgives without paying a price himself for the offense of another. To forgive a person who has wronged you means that you release him and in fact bear your own vexation of his trespass. Bearing your own wrath on another's offense means that you do not disgrace him. Only then does redemption become possible.

God reveals such wrath-bearing at Calvary. In Christ, He bore all of our sin, absorbed our hatred into himself, even unto death. Dying on the cross, Jesus returned words of love and pardon. He carried His own wrath on our sin—paying the real cost of forgiveness.

Myron Augsburger notes in his book, *Faith for a Secular World*, these poignant lines:[2]

> To forgive is costly, to carry one's own wrath
> On the sin of another;
> The guilty one is released,
> The offended frees him, by
> Bearing his own indignation
> And resolving it in love.
> God forgives by carrying His own wrath
> On the sin we've expressed against Him;
> The depth of our guilt is seen at the Cross,
> The greatness of His love matched it, for
> "He bare our sins in His own body,"
> He absorbs our guilt and makes us free.
> Forgiveness goes through the sin to freedom.

The cross of Christ was indeed the instrument through which the eternal love of God became revealed in forgiveness to this world of sinners. On the middle cross, splitting human history, the divine Son expressed the forgiveness burning in God's heart from the dawn of creation. He invites us now to come to Him and be freed, released from our estrangement and guilt. He will forgive and accept us, remake us after His will.

How often, in our humanness and pride, we only express tolerance in our relationships. Instead of forgiving and releasing the offender, we just tolerate him. Our tolerance becomes the ultimate expression of pride, which is an insult to the other person. Tolerance implies one should be satisfied if you permit him in your presence even though you keep him at your feet. Such attitudes create personal problems, foment class struggle, racial strife, and international hostilities.[3]

Jesus' response to His disciples' quest for greatness was to call for a conversion to a childlike spirit. Such a spirit reminds us how dependent we are on each other. Setting a little child in their midst, Jesus said, "I tell you the truth, unless you change and become like little children, you will never enter the kingdom of heaven . . . .whoever humbles himself like this child is the greatest in the kingdom of heaven" (Matt. 18:3-4).

Unless we deal frankly with our own sins, we will condemn others. Paul declares, "Bear with each other and forgive whatever grievances you may have against one another. Forgive as the Lord forgave you" (Col. 3:13). An honest admission of our own faults prompts us to forgive others who stumble. As we acknowledge our failures along with those of others, this avowal allows our inner self the joy of forgiveness. To forgive oneself means we accept the humbling truth that we are less than ideal, calling us to repentance and new life.

To tolerate a person in lieu of forgiving harbors the basic malice. Christian faith takes hold of a new union, a fellowship of the forgiven. We need to live in the common assent that all believers are forgiven sinners, that every sinner is one for whom Christ died. Though tolerance may respect another's place and faith, it doesn't offer the living covenant of common commitment to God. His covenant people transcend racial ties or some exclusive club of members. They are the redeemed of the ages—the Church.

Forgiveness only functions in relationship. It is not a commodity one can corner. Again, forgiveness requires acceptance of the guilty person at a cost to the forgiving one. This becomes included in the meaning of the Cross, "Restoration of fellowship, whether with God or among men, can only be at a cost. Here no force is more creative or more potent in its effects than victorious suffering. In human relationships no less than in God's dealings with men, to love is to suffer, and to suffer is to love."[4]

Edwin Markham, a poet, became persuaded by some friends to put his lifetime savings into unsound investments. One day he learned that he had lost everything. At first, strong resentment swept over him, flooding his soul. But not for long. His deep Christian faith prevailed. He took a sheet of paper, drew two circles, and quickly wrote his famous quatrain, "Outwitted":

> He drew a circle that shut me out—
> Heretic, rebel, a thing to flout,
> But love and I had the wit to win:
> We drew a circle that took him in.[5]

Love and forgiveness cannot be divorced. Interpersonal relations always involve the acceptance of imperfect people. Love enables one to forgive another who has done wrong. In love, the forgiving one carries his own wrath on the other's trespass, freeing the guilty. A person who forgives doesn't humiliate the culprit first, and then accept him. That would not be forgiveness—it would only pamper one's ego and dismiss the case.

The price of forgiveness includes resolving within oneself, by love, the anger another's wrong provokes. That person becomes accepted in freedom. Those forgiven know they become approved because of another's grace. So the Psalmist declared, "But there is forgiveness with Thee, That Thou mayest be feared" (130:4, NASB).

Knowing our own faults, we realize we can only enjoy new life with God if He really forgives! Proof that God for Christ's sake has forgiven us is in the gift of the Holy Spirit. God's Spirit comes to abide in us to fulfill the Divine promise. To the crowd at Pentecost, Peter said, "Repent and be baptized, every one of you, in the name of Jesus Christ for the forgiveness of your sins. And you will receive the gift of the Holy Spirit" (Acts 2:38).

Paul later wrote to believers at Corinth that since Christ purchased their redemption by His blood on Calvary, they belonged to God. Their very bodies must be the temple of the Holy Spirit (cf. 1 Cor. 2:2; 3:16). Christians today realize the ultimate expression of salvation is God dwelling in the midst of His people. Our reconciliation with God has this inner witness, the present indwelling of the Holy Spirit. He testifies to our spirits that we have been adopted as sons and daughters into God's family. He affirms the joy of forgiveness and rejects any notion of tolerance within the union.

Forgiveness seems too hard and out of reach if one consults only the natural heart. A rebellious, sinful nature has no taste for this joy, and will never attain it within itself. But in union with the Spirit of Christ, we find the joy of forgiveness as well as the love to forgive others. Those who abide in Christ become strengthened to walk even as He walked.

The Healing of Love

The first and basic healing Jesus Christ brings to us is forgiveness of our sins. Our repentance and God's forgiveness remain at the heart of Christian doctrine. Because God so loved us, He sent His only begotten Son to die for our sins, and whoever believes in Him will have everlasting life (John 3:16). When we repent and believe in Christ's great love for us, we find salvation and healing at the inmost level of our beings.

In turn, when we love, we forgive. We forget grudges and show mercy; we serve God in the beauty of holiness. Truly preaching the good news of salvation is not just telling people, but impacting the Word of truth on individual lives. No amount of talk will ever convince them of the love of the Father. The words must effect action that enters their private realm. Ours must be a personal ministry that responds to the needs of others with loving concern.

God revealed himself as loving Healer in the person of His Son, Jesus Christ. Only His loyal disciples can truly preach Christ. You and I cannot reveal the Holy One by simply talking about holiness. We can disclose Him only by being holy in our conduct. We can be holy in our daily living only as we by faith are filled with His love. So Daniel Steele, in his *Milestone Papers*, said, "Let all the forces in the soul of the justified person wheel into line with the dominant force, love to God; then the soul mounts swiftly upward, like a balloon when the ropes are all cut and the sandbags are all cast out."[6]

As we follow Christ, taking up our cross daily, He enables us by His Holy Spirit to fulfill His loving purpose in our lives. Our sinful nature becomes crucified with Christ, and by faith His Spirit fills our hearts with His love. Under the glow of God's redeeming love, we behold the glory of His forgiveness through Jesus' blood. His loving pardon applies healing to all of sin's diseases.

No question can remain whether we should forgive others. When our hearts become filled with the love of Christ, we will obey God, and love our fellowmen—even our enemies, or those that are repulsive to us. A heart full of love finds it blessed to forgive—a boon to happiness and inner health. We become empowered to resist the temptation not to forgive those who have hurt or wronged us.

Living in God's forgiving love opens our lives to allow its beautiful light to shine through us and on others. This fosters the healing of damaged relationships. The prophet says, " . . . for you who revere my name, the sun of righteousness will rise with healing in its wings" (Mal. 4:2).

A scientist looks at the sunlight shining down on a filthy street. He imagines all sorts of germs dying by the millions in the bright rays. Lab experiments have proved sunlight is a great germ-destroyer. No bacillus known can survive it. Truly the sun has healing in its wings. So Jesus Christ, "the sun of righteousness," heals the diseases of mankind. Our sinful moral nature revives to health in His presence. No evil can survive the sunlight of God's love aglow in the hearts of believers.

Christ is indeed the world's healer—the Great Physician. He remains present in the sickroom, and at work for our spiritual welfare. A celebrated doctor who always entered a patient's room with a smile was asked how he could deal with so many terrible afflictions and not be overwhelmed by them. he replied, "I always look upon disease from a curative standpoint."

That is the distinct approach of our Lord. Even from the Cross, dying as the final Sacrifice for our sin, Jesus looked on sin-sick humanity from the curative standpoint. Through faith in the Savior, we too can view our personal relationship problems with hopes of healing. As we walk in the light of His love and truth we experience the all-sufficiency of His sustaining grace. His indwelling presence supplies us with love that forgives and redeems. We become empowered to forgive even as Christ has forgiven us.

Scriptural truth relates how the forgiveness of sins impacts bodily and emotional illness. Though not all physical disease is the direct result of sin, Jesus knew the frequent relationship. In the account of the paralytic whose friends let him down through the roof, Jesus first forgave the man's sins before He told him to pick up his cot and walk (Luke 4:20).

The Apostle connects some sickness and death in the Corinthian church to faulty relationships with God and other people. No Christian

Forgiveness Heals the Hopeless

should attempt holy communion with unsettled grievances or unconfessed sin lurking in his heart. Paul calls for proper observance of the Lord's Supper. "For anyone who eats and drinks without recognizing the body of the Lord eats and drinks judgment on himself. That is why many among you are weak and sick, and a number of you have fallen asleep" (1 Cor. 11:29-30).

Though sickness and death befall all Christians, we should seek the blessing of right relationships. Much illness within the Church today exists because people have strayed from unity with God, and are at odds with their neighbors. The healing of God's love must flow. The soothing balm of the Holy Spirit of Christ will ease the friction as we seek to obey His loving will.

One of Satan's clever tricks it to prod well-meaning people into thinking that petty differences among Christians do not hamper love's free flow. The crisis experiences of regeneration and entire sanctification will soon lose their glow unless we daily confess God's forgiving and cleansing love. Neither can we be redemptive lights in this lost sin-darkened world. Both our personal progress and Christian witness become stymied.

Dr. Paul Tournier, well-known physician, broadened the merely physical treatment of his patients. He increased his own prayer life and studied psychology so he could help the sick person find healing at all levels of his being. One finds it helpful—even essential—to pray in repentance or for inner healing before praying for physical healing.

Surprisingly, we see Jesus in Scripture as rebuking the unforgiving more than crying out against fleshly sins. Again and again, we become struck by the way He connects the Father's forgiving and answering our prayers with our forgiveness of our enemies. "And when you stand praying, if you hold anything against anyone, forgive him, so that your Father in heaven may forgive you your sins" (Mark 11:25).

The "bottom line" is that divine love remains the key to healing, both spiritual and physical. Where would we be without God's forgiving kiss of love? How effective will our Christian witness be unless we apply that healing seal to those bound by hate?

A Christian lady once worked among the moral strays of London. She found a prostitute lying in a dank, bare room, desperately ill. She tried to minister to the girl, changing her filthy bed linen, and making the shabby quarters as livable as possible. She also offered food and medicine to the girl. Then the lady asked, "May I pray with you?"

"No," sneered the girl, "You don't care for me—you're just doing this because you think it'll help you get to heaven."

Days passed. The Christian woman returned often in helpful kindness. But the street girl remained hard and bitter. At last, the Christian said, "You are nearly well now, so I shall not come again. Since this is my last visit, I would like for you to let me kiss you."

Holy forgiving lips prayerfully met those lips that had been defiled by vile oaths and fleshly lust. The hard heart broke. It showed Christ's way. Love, true forgiving love, conquered where mere service without love would have been only a "clanging cymbal," calling attention to itself.[7]

Nothing characterizes love more than forgiveness. Its virtue provides total healing. Through the love of God in Christ Jesus we become whole, redeemed persons, forgiven and cleansed from all sin. No wonder John Wesley defined the imparted fullness of the Holy Spirit upon believers in terms of "perfect love!"

Wesley said Christian perfection had various aspects. "It is purity of intention, dedicating all the life to God." It includes also "the circumcision of the heart from all filthiness, all inward as well as outward pollution." The Christian fullness becomes described as "the loving God with all our heart and our neighbor as ourselves."[8]

Holiness Means Wholeness

Some have supposed God does not want us to be holy like Him until death. Such a concept infers He allows us to be unholy until we die. The truth is: God does not want us to be unholy anytime. Many Christians in the past attached evil to the human body. But God's outpoured love through Jesus' life, death, and resurrection in the flesh provides the means whereby the whole life of a person can be made holy.

Holiness is indeed wholeness. It does not refer to fragmented righteousness of the spirit and sinfulness of the flesh. Instead, it means a spiritual health that includes the total person as he relates to God and to other people. This holiness of character, attitudes, and action does not spring from innate human goodness, but it depends upon the love we receive from God by faith.

Around 1650, Jeremy Taylor wrote:

Love is the greatest thing that God can give us; for Himself is love: and it is the greatest thing we can give to God; for it will also give ourselves, and carry with it all that is ours. The apostle calls it the bond of perfection; it is the old, and it is the new, and it is the great commandment; and it is all the commandments; for it is the fulfilling of the law.[9]

Paul speaks of Christians perfecting holiness as a progressive work. "Since we have these promises, . . . let us purify ourselves, . . . and let us strive for perfection out of reverence for God" (2 Cor. 7:1). We must put into practice the cleansing from all rebellion against God instantaneously wrought within by the Spirit of Christ.

One eminent proponent of Christian purity for a year kept on smoking cigars and invoked divine blessing on them as sincerely as he did his meal. But as he progressed walking in the light of divine truth, that piercing judgment showed him the harm the habit inflicted to him and to the cause of Christ. His conscience banished that marring poison forever from his lips.[10]

How blind we often are to our own shortcomings that seem so obvious to others. Most of us, at some time or other, become aware of idols in our hearts we once overlooked. The Holy Spirit of Christ remains faithful to reveal them to us as we walk in the light of His truth. Here, again, is reason for saying daily, "Forgive us our trespasses." Truly, there is no person, however pure, whose increased knowledge may not see in his past conduct, acts or omissions, that do not jibe with the standard of perfect righteousness.

Because the moral eye remains too dull to see such shortcomings, the very possibility that one is an unconscious transgressor should send him to the Blood-sprinkled mercy seat of Christ. We should exclaim with Paul, "My conscience is clear, but that does not make me innocent. It is the Lord who judges me" (1 Cor. 4:4).

Bishop Butler once remarked that God could not possibly create a moral being with good habits. He further said we don't know how far it becomes possible in the nature of things that effects become wrought in us at once equivalent to habits. So if, through grace, we become fortified by virtuous habits, we should thank God for an estate, better in at least one respect, than Adam's when "freshest from the hand of God."[11]

Daniel Steele notes several important inferences from Butler's remarks:[12]

1. Finding in our acts any lack of conformity to the law of love, made after entire sanctification by our increasing moral insight, is not proof of inbred sin still lurking within our hearts. All our inward impulses may be Godward, and the blood of His Son, Jesus Christ, may be cleansing us from all sin.

2. Many believers, who have made complete consecration and received the fullness of the sanctifying Spirit, have found their moral vision still faulty. They may fail to give glory to the Sanctifier for His great work, and slip back into their former confused state of sinning and repenting.

3. Here is grounds for the so-called Wesleyan paradox, that entire sanctification is both instantaneous and gradual. In the impulsive power imparted to the believer's conscience, it is instantaneous; in the discerning power of the moral sense, through practice, it is gradual. Paul calls for both aspects in 2 Corinthians 7:1.

In the baptism with the Holy Spirit, with the fullness of His cleansing and the infilling of His perfect love, He comes as our abiding Comforter. This work of entire sanctification is instantaneous as was the revelation of Christ in Paul after his justification (Gal. 1:15-16). The Apostle's prayers for entire sanctification imply a distinct work, set in time, and followed by certain wholesome effects called fruits.

Paul prays for the complete faith of believers (1 Thess. 3:9-13). He prays that saints might be filled with divine fullness (Eph. 3:14-21). He prays that believers might be filled with "the fruit of righteousness" (Phil.

1:9-11). And he specifically prays, "May God himself, the God of peace, sanctify you through and through" (1 Thess. 5:23).

The writer of the Epistle to the Hebrews intimates that Christian perfection becomes reached in the process of time in the development of moral vision. Speaking from the spiritual aspect, he says, "But solid food is for the mature, who because of practice have their senses trained to discern good and evil" (5:14, NASB).

Here the words "practice" and "trained" imply a gradual sanctification in the only realm appropriate for it—in the power of moral discernment. The unfolding of moral insight under an ever-increasing knowledge is a work that remains to be done. Because of the incompleteness of this work at any given point in his life, a person may say of his life and practice, "sanctified up to knowledge." But respecting his heart he may say, "sanctified wholly," throughout the conscious and unconscious realm of soul and spirit.

The sanctifying Spirit of Christ, by His powerful and instantaneous inworking, corrects the will, poises the passions aright, controls all innocent and removes all unholy desires. The Lord is enthroned over a realm in which no rebel hides. The Holy Spirit gives witness to this holy work although one's knowledge remains imperfect. Our "wholeness" depends on His leadership. The Spirit's guidance shows deliverance from the slavery of sin, as the ground of justification, as the impulse to serve God, throughout our lives. He is the abiding agent of our sanctification.

The inspired writers of Scripture relate the thought of healing, particularly for a person's heart. In the Old Testament, Isaiah said, "The whole head is sick, and the whole heart is faint" (1:5, NASB). Jeremiah declared, "The heart is more deceitful than all else and is desperately sick; . . . " (17:9, NASB). Also, the prophet said, " . . . they have healed the brokenness of my people superficially, . . . " (Jer. 6:14).

Sin, inherited depravity, makes the heart sick. The Lord Jesus Christ came to heal a world of lost sinners. The apostle Peter declares, "He himself bore our sins in his body on the cross, so that we might die to sins and live for righteousness; by his wounds you have been healed" (1 Pet. 2:24).

This primarily refers to mankind's common spiritual disease, not to physical ailments. However, our conscience finds healing in Christ's wounds. Our will receives healing by His sufferings; our cluttered affections become healed by His passion. The Lord's wounds heal our desires, and the fountain of our thoughts becomes healed by the blood that flowed from His veins.[13]

Mrs. Hester Ann Rogers, one of John Wesley's faithful helpers, wrote to a friend:

> It is the blood of Jesus that cleanseth from all sin, not penal sufferings, not mortification of any kind, not anything we have, not grace already received, not anything we are or can be, not death nor purgatory, no, nor the purgatory of all doings and sufferings, and strivings put together . . . Christ is the procuring meritorious cause of all our salvation. He alone forgiveth sin and He alone cleanseth from all unrighteousness . . . ."[14]

Our faith holds the only condition to share the holy power of the One it dares to trust. May we not "receive the grace of god in vain" (2 Cor. 6:1). Let us hasten to plunge, as it were, into the fountain that became opened for sin and uncleanness (Zech. 13:1). Indeed, we should not be satisfied until the wounds of Christ become applied in making us perfectly whole. Say with the Apostle, "May I never boast except in the cross of our Lord Jesus Christ, through which the world has been crucified to me, and I to the world" (Gal. 6:14).

Christ's cross remains our point of contact for wholeness. Our prayer for healing seeks to know the common sensation of heat, that feeling linked with human love, the warmth of friendship. Heat and cold symbolize love and hate; they suggest God's total healing and its opposite, the death wish of Satan. The warmth of love must overcome the cold of hatred for God's healing to result. A life cold to the Divine will marks the presence of evil. Life and death thus become locked in conflict within our beings.

Often, spiritual or physical healing becomes blocked by our coldness, our resentment and lack of forgiveness. No wonder James, in his passage on praying for the sick with anointing, also encourages confession of sins:

"Therefore, confess your sins to each other and pray for each other so that you may be healed. The prayer of a righteous man is powerful and effective" (James 5:16).

Christians have long known the power of Jesus Christ to forgive sins. The gospel of God invites all who languish in hopelessness to pray for healing. Often there exists a close interrelation between all forms of healing. One's wholeness overlaps both physical and spiritual health. In fact a person can be sick unto death and be spiritually whole. But an illness may stem from the spiritual level, affecting one's physical health.

Physical, as well as spiritual healing, often requires first a forgiveness of sin, an inner healing, before wholeness can pervade. For instance, the most vital repentance rises from bitterness, resentment, an affliction Christians sometimes fail to see in themselves. God's love is the only remedy to break through the coldness, the sin, the hurt and rancor that block His healing power flowing into us and making us whole.

Our most basic need is to know we are loved—not for anything we can do or achieve, but simply because we are. "But God demonstrates his own love for us in this: While we were still sinners, Christ died for us" (Rom. 5:8). Believers cling to such redeeming love forever. But the hopeless have never really grasped God's love. Jesus Christ, by His Spirit, shows how much He cares for each person by healing individual hurts that have broken our hearts and withered our spirits. Thank God, He still works in the soul-restoring business!

Confess your need and receive the Savior's holy kiss of forgiveness. The Lord Jesus fulfills Isaiah's prophecy: "In his name the nations will put their hope" (Matt. 12:21). In Christlike obedience we find the true joy of divine love. It secures bold access into God's presence. The reality of His love confirms the full sweep of His everlasting forgiveness and cleansing.

The Scripture assures us, time and again, that God wills to blot out our sins and to remember them against us no more. Doubting hearts ask: "How can we know our sins have been forgiven? How can we know our sinful nature has been purged?"

The repeated scriptural answer is: "By the witness of the Spirit." It is as though God's voice speaks peace to one's soul, assuring him of His forgiveness. Charles Wesley describes the experience in his hymn. "All Things are Ready":[15]

> 1. Sinners, obey the gospel word;
> Haste to the supper of my Lord;
> Be wise to know your gracious day;
> All things are ready,—come away.
>
> 2. Ready the Father is to own
> And kiss his late-returning son;
> Ready your loving Savior stands,
> And spreads for you his bleeding hands.
>
> 3. Ready the Spirit of his love,
> Just now the stony to remove;
> To apply and witness with the blood,
> And wash and seal the sons of God.
>
> 5. The Father, Son, and Holy Ghost,
> Are ready, with their shining host;
> All heaven is ready to resound,
> "The dead's alive! the lost is found!"

NOTES

1. T. A. Kantonen, *Theology of Evangelism*, 78.

2. Myron S. Augsburger, *Faith for a Secular World* (Waco, Tex.: Word Books, Publishers, 1968), 61.

3. Cf. Ibid., 62.

4. Cited in Ibid., 63.

5. A. Gordon Nasby (ed.), *1041 Sermon Illustrations, Ideas, and Expositions*, 208.

6. Daniel Steele, *Hints for Holy Living*, 36.

7. Cf. Walter B. Knight, *Knight's Master Book of New Illustrations*, 397.

8. John Wesley, *Works*, XI, 444.

9. Jeremy Taylor, *The Rule and Exercise of Holy Living* (New York: Harper and Row, Publishers, reprint 1970), 111.

10. Daniel Steele, *Hints for Holy Living*, 38-39.

11. Ibid., 40.

12. Cf. Ibid.

13. A. Paget Wilkes, *Dynamic of Redemption*, 79.

14. Cited in Ibid., 81.

15. *Hymnal of the Methodist Episcopal Church*, 212.

Bibliography

I. BOOKS

AGNEW, MILTON S. *More than Conquerors*. Chicago: Salvation Army, 1959.

AUGSBURGER, MYRON S. *Faith for a Secular World*. Waco, Tex.: Word Books Publishers, 1968.

AUGUSTINE. *Confessions*.

BAXTER, RICHARD. *The Saints' Everlasting Rest*. New York: American Tract Society, n.d.

BROCKETT, HENRY E. *The Christian and Romans 7*. Kansas City: Beacon Hill Press, 1972.

BUNYAN, JOHN. *Grace Abounding*. Chicago: Moody Press, 1959.

———. *The Pilgrim's Progress*. New York: Books, Inc., 1946.

CHAMBERS, OSWALD. *Conformed to His Image*. London: Marshall, Morgan, & Scott, Ltd., 1955.

———. *The Philosophy of Sin*. London: Simkin Marshall, 1941.

———. *The Psychology of Redemption*. London: Marshall, Morgan, & Scott, Ltd., 1955.

COLEMAN, ROBERT E. *Written in Blood*. Old Tappan, N.J.: Fleming H. Revell Co., 1972.

CURTIS, OLIN A. *The Christian Faith*. Grand Rapids: Kregel Publications, 1956.

DAVIDSON, A. B. *The Theology of the Old Testament*. New York: Charles Scribner's Sons, 1917.

DILLISTONE, F. W. *Jesus Christ and His Cross*. Philadelphia: The Westminster Press, 1953.

DOAN, ELEANOR L. (comp.). *431 Quotes from the Notes of Henrietta C. Mears*. Glendale, Calif.: 1970.

Expositor's Bible, Second Epistle to the Corintians.

FORSYTH, P. T. *The Justified God*. Independent Press, 1857.

———. *The Work of Christ*. Collins, 1865.

———. *God the Holy Father*. Independent Press, 1959.

———. *The Cruciality of the Cross*. Grand Rapids: William B. Eerdmans Publishing Co., n.d.

———. *The Christian Ethic of War*. New York: Longman's, Green. 1917.

———. *Church and Sacraments*.

———. *The Gospel and Authority*. Minneapolis: Augsburg Publishing House, 1971.

GORDON, S. D. *Quiet Talks with World Winners*. New York: Fleming H. Revell Co., 1908.

GREATHOUSE, WILLIAM M. *The Fullness of the Spirit*. Kansas City: Nazarene Publishing House, 1958.

HALLOCK, G. B. F. *2500 Best Modern Illustrations*. New York: Harper & Brothers Publishers, 1935.

HAVERGAL FRANCES RIDLEY. *Kept for the Master's Use*. Chicago: Donohue, Henneberry & Co., 1879.

HAZELTON, ROGER. *Renewing the Mind*. New York: The MacMillan Co., 1949.

HOWARD, RICHARD E. *Newness of Life*. Kansas City: Beacon Hill Press, 1975.

HUNTER, A. M. *P. T. Forsyth*. Philadelphia: Westminster Press, 1954.

Hymnal of the Methodist Episcopal Church. New York: Nelson & Phillips, 1878.

KANTONEN, T. A. *Theology of Evangelism*. Philadelphia: Muhlenberg Press, 1954.
KIERKEGAARD, SOREN. *Journals*.
KNIGHT, WALTER B. *Master Book of New Illustrations*. Grand Rapids: Wm. B. Eermans Publishing Co., 1970.
MANTLE, JOHN GREGORY. *Beyond Humiliation*. Chicago: Moody Press, n.d.
MEAD, FRANK S. (ed.). *The Encyclopedia of Religious Quotations*. Old Tappan, N.J.: Spire Books. 1976.
METZ, DONALD. *Studies of Biblical Holiness*. Kansas City: Beacon Hill Press, 1971.
MILEY, JOHN. *Systematic Theology*. New York: Hunt & Eaton, 1892.
MORGAN, G. CAMPBELL. *The Crises of the Christ*. Louisville, Ky.: Pentecostal Publishing Co., 1903.
MORRISON, J. G. *Our Lost Estate*. Kansas City: Nazarene Publishing House, 1929.
MURRAY, ANDREW. *Like Christ*. New York: Fleming H. Revell Co., n.d.
NASBY, A. GORDON (e.d.). *1041 Sermon Illustrations, Ideas, and Expositions*. Grand Rapids: Baker Book House, 1976.
OUTLER, ALBERT C. *Theology in the Wesleyan Spirit*. Nashville: Tidings, 1975.
PANNENBERG, WOLFHART. *What Is Man? Contemporary Anthropology in Theological Perspective*. Translated by Duane A. Prisbe. Philadelphia: Fortress Press, 1970.
PURKISER, W. T. (e.d.). *Exploring Our Christian Faith*. Kansas City: Beacon Hill Press, 1964.
RALSTON, THOMAS N. *Elements of Divinity*. Nashville: Southern Methodist Publishing House, 1876.
SANDERS, J. OSWALD. *Cultivation of Christian Culture*. Chicago: Moody Press, 1965.
SMALL, DWIGHT HERVEY. *The High Cost of Holy Living*. Westwood, N. J.: Fleming H. Revell Co., 1964.
STEELE, DANIEL. *Hints for Holy Living*. Kansas City: Beacon Hill Press, 1959.
STEWART, JAMES S. *A Faith to Proclaim*. New York: Charles Scribner's Sons, 1953.
——————. *A Man in Christ*. New York: Harper & Row, n.d.
TAN, PAUL LEE. *Encyclopedia of 7700 Illustrations*. Rockville, Md.: Assurance Publishers, 1984.
TAYLOR, JEREMY. *The Rule and Exercise of Holy Living*. New York: Harper & Row, Publishers, reprint, 1970.
WESLEY, JOHN. *Plain Account of Christian Perfection*. Chicago: Free Methodist Publishing House, n.d.
——————. *Works*. Grand Rapids: Zondervan Publishing House, n.d.
WHITEHEAD, ALFRED NORTH. *Adventures of Ideas*. New York: Macmillan Co., 1933.
WILEY, H. ORTON. *Christian Theology*. Kansas City: Beacon Hill Press, 1953.
——————, and CULTBERTSON, PAUL T. *Introduction to Christian Theology*. Kansas City: Beacon Hill Press, 1957.
WILKES, A. PAGET. *The Dynamic of Redemption*. Kansas City: Beacon Hill Press, 1954.

II. ARTICLES

Jubilee. The Monthly Newsletter of Prison Fellowship, February, 1985.
PURKISER, W. T. "The Two Meanings of Grace," *Herald of Holiness*, May 21, 1975.